MURDER & MAYHEM
— IN —
SOUTHWESTERN
ILLINOIS

JOHN J. DUNPHY

THE
History
PRESS

Published by The History Press
Charleston, SC
www.historypress.com

Unless otherwise noted, all photos were taken by the author.

First published 2021

Manufactured in the United States

ISBN 9781467147910

Library of Congress Control Number: 2020945765

Notice: The information in this book is true and complete to the best of our knowledge. It is offered without guarantee on the part of the author or The History Press. The author and The History Press disclaim all liability in connection with the use of this book.

For Loretta

CONTENTS

ACKNOWLEDGEMENTS

All photographs were taken by me, except where credited otherwise in the captions. I owe such a debt to Sharon Schaefer of Hayner Public Library in Alton, who is always willing to help me find old newspaper accounts that complement my research. William P. Shannon IV, curator of the St. Clair County Historical Society, located some newspaper articles detailing the grisly facts of David Wyatt's lynching. The Archival Library of the Madison County Historical Society in Edwardsville is a treasure-trove of historical material. My appreciation to the Alton Museum of History and Art for graciously allowing me to photograph the original tombstone of the Wood River Massacre victims.

And thank you, Alluriana, for being such an avid reader of my published works. I hope you enjoy this book.

INTRODUCTION

Books dealing with historical violence generally tend to focus on wars and revolutions. Not this book. With the exception of the Illinois National Guard during the East St. Louis race riot, the violent incidents chronicled within these pages were committed by civilians, not soldiers or revolutionaries. Many of these residents of southwestern Illinois could have been my neighbors and friends had I been living at the time.

These incidents are in no way what are typically referred to as "random acts of violence." They mirrored the social and political climate of our nation at the time they occurred. My region's history is America's history. The Wood River Massacre occurred during the War of 1812, when the British encouraged Native Americans to attack pioneer settlements. The horrendous abuse inflicted on a slave in Edwardsville and the crowd of local residents that attended the hanging of a Black abolitionist remind us that barbaric treatment of Black people in pre–Civil War America was by no means limited to the South. The lynching of a Black schoolteacher in 1903 and the 1917 race riot in East St. Louis indicate the pervasiveness of racism in the twentieth-century United States. It's a tragic irony that these incidents occurred in the state that sent Lincoln to the White House and received acclaim for being the first state to ratify the Thirteenth Amendment, which abolished slavery.

Speaking of Lincoln, this book includes one of the most bizarre incidents in the life of our nation's greatest president: his duel with another Illinois politician on a Mississippi River island opposite the city of Alton. This account stands in stark contrast to an earlier chapter that deals with the first duel held in the Prairie State. The loser of that duel, which was held in Belleville, died from a gunshot wound. The winner of that duel died on the gallows.

Readers will surely be surprised to see a chapter on the celebrated pirate Jean Lafitte in a book dealing with the history of southwestern Illinois. The beginning of that chapter will correct the misconception that piracy was confined to the high seas. Pirates plied their nefarious trade on inland waters as well, including the Mississippi River. And they continued to plunder shore-dwellers even in the twentieth century.

The lawlessness of Benbow City is more reminiscent of a town in the nineteenth-century Wild West than a twentieth-century community in southwestern Illinois. I avoided chronicling the malefactions of gun-toting gangsters, since I regard them as outside the scope of this book. Nonetheless, I felt obligated to include a chapter on Curtis Reese, who served as pastor of Alton's First Unitarian Church and battled this region's underworld. After leaving southwestern Illinois, Reese became one of the giants of the humanist movement. He signed the original Humanist Manifesto in 1933 and served as director of the Abraham Lincoln Center for almost three decades.

The victim of the 1903 lynching was murdered because of his race. The victim of the 1918 lynching lost his life because of his nationality. During World War I, anti-German hysteria engulfed the United States. Numerous Americans of German descent were persecuted for their ethnicity. Only one was murdered, however, and that crime was committed here in southwestern Illinois.

It's a common misconception that the Ku Klux Klan limited its activity to the southern states. That infamous organization achieved a level of nationwide success during the 1920s that can only be described as astonishing. The KKK had a strong presence in southwestern Illinois. While racist and anti-Semitic, the Klan's primary focus at that time was anti-Catholicism. The author's great-uncle, who is featured prominently in his earlier book for Arcadia/History Press *From Christmas to Twelfth Night in Southern Illinois*, participated in an anti-Klan rally that was held while the KKK burned a cross.

The Ku Klux Klan enjoyed a brief resurgence in the 1990s in my region. I'm proud to have participated in the anti-Klan struggle and recount my experiences in this book.

My hometown of Alton takes pride in being the birthplace of Miles Davis, the jazz musician, and Robert Wadlow, the tallest human being of all time. We often refrain from mentioning that Alton is also the birthplace of James Earl Ray, who assassinated Dr. Martin Luther King Jr. Readers will be surprised to learn that Ray was a petty criminal in this region before attaining celebrity status by killing our nation's greatest civil rights leader. The author's grandmother was shopping in the grocery store located next to her home when Ray burst in to rob the place.

We baby boomers grew up during the Cold War. From watching TV footage of nuclear weapons tests to classroom drills that had us cowering under our desks to teach us how to react in the event of an enemy attack, the tension between our nation and the old Soviet Union was always part of our lives. Southwestern Illinois played an active role in the Cold War when it was chosen as the site of a Nike missile base.

The base was located in Pere Marquette State Park, which is surely one of the most beautiful state parks in Illinois. Located on the Illinois River and sporting a magnificent lodge built by the Civilian Conservation Corps, the park's terrain includes densely wooded hills, hiking trails and Indian mounds. The ruins of the Nike base can still be seen, a Cold War relic that nature has been slowly reclaiming for decades.

The incidents chronicled in this book occurred during the nineteenth and twentieth centuries. No event that has occurred in the twenty-first century even remotely qualified for inclusion in this book. But the twenty-first century is still very young.

THE WOOD RIVER MASSACRE

Situated along present-day Illinois Route 140 in Madison County, the Wood River Settlement was one of the earliest pioneer communities in southwestern Illinois. This settlement, which consisted of a few widely dispersed log cabins, was the site of the Wood River Massacre in 1814, when a woman and six children were murdered by members of the Kickapoo tribe. Two of the victims were the oldest children of Abel and Mary (Bates) Moore. This tragedy, the worst Indian depredation that southern Illinois suffered during the War of 1812—when the British urged tribes to attack American settlements—marked the last Native American reprisal against pioneers in Madison County.

The Wood River Massacre occurred on Rattan's Prairie, which included the land between the east and west forks of the Wood River. Rattan's Prairie was named for Thomas Rattan, an Ohioan who settled in the area in 1804. The two forks unite a short distance south of Rattan's Prairie, and the Wood River meanders its way to the Mississippi. Lewis and Clark established Camp River Dubois at the mouth of the Wood River in 1803 and wintered there before embarking on their epic journey west in the spring of 1804. The fertile soil between the Wood River forks attracted other pioneer families, and a small community known as the Wood River Settlement took root.

The Moore family, which included Abel and Mary Bates Moore, relocated from North Carolina to Kentucky in 1802. According to research conducted by the General George Rogers Clark Chapter of the Sons of the American Revolution (SAR), which serves Madison and four other Illinois counties, this move was prompted by the friendship of the Moore and Bates families with Daniel Boone.

In the spring of 1808, the Moores began another journey under Boone's leadership, this time for Missouri. Abel and Mary were accompanied by their two children as well as Abel's father, John Moore, and Mary's father, William Bates, both of whom were veterans of the American Revolution. According to the SAR, Bates served as a private in the First South Carolina Regiment commanded by Colonel Charles Pinckney. He also served as a spy for Colonel Abraham Sheppard.

The party also included Abel's brothers, George and William, as well as the family of William Bates. Upon reaching Ford's Ferry on the Ohio River, Abel and Mary Moore, their children and the Bates family parted company with Boone and decided to journey to the Illinois country. John Moore and his two other sons traveled on to Boone's Lick, Missouri, where John soon died.

Abel, Mary, their children and the Bates family eventually reached the present-day site of East Alton in Madison County. Abel "pitched his tent, but was so annoyed by the mosquitoes that he removed to a higher elevation, where later he improved a farm," according to an 1894 Madison County history. That higher elevation was Rattan's Prairie. The three Moore brothers evidently had made a pact to reunite following the death of their father. Abel Moore built a signal fire on the bank of the Wood River every day for two years to let George, William and their families know his location. The brothers were overjoyed upon finally reuniting. The Reagan family, which was also destined to play a major role in the settlement's history, arrived at Rattan's Prairie with the party of George and William Moore. The Moores were such a strong presence in this pioneer community that it was sometimes referred to as Moore's Settlement.

On Sunday, July 10, 1814, Reason Reagan decided to walk the three-mile distance from his home at the Wood River Settlement to the nearest church, which was a Baptist congregation that met near the present location of the Vaughn Hill Cemetery. He left his wife, Rachel, and their two children—seven-year-old Elizabeth, nicknamed Betsy, and three-year-old Timothy—at the cabin of Abel and Mary Moore, where he thought they would be safe. According to Tom Emery, who researched this event, Rachel was pregnant at the time. Abel Moore was then at nearby Fort Russell. Most adult male residents of the Wood River Settlement served in the Territorial Rangers. Abel Moore had attained the rank of captain. Both his brothers were accomplished gunmakers and supplied the Territorial Rangers with firearms.

The grave site of Abel and Mary Moore. The small tombstone in the foreground is their original grave marker.

At about 4:00 p.m., Rachel Reagan started home with Elizabeth and Timothy. She also took with her eleven-year-old Joel and eight-year-old William Moore, as well as the two children of William Moore, their uncle: John, age ten, and George, age three. Rachel wanted to harvest some fresh green beans from her garden to serve with the Sunday supper that was to be held at the cabin of Abel and Mary Moore. An eighth person began the journey to the Reagan cabin, fifteen-year-old Hannah Bates, the sister of Mary Bates Moore, but she developed a painful blister on her foot and returned to the Moore cabin. It was later determined that the teenager turned back less than three hundred yards from where Rachel Reagan's body was discovered. Several men, who were walking through the vicinity about the time that Rachel Reagan and the six children left the Moore cabin, later stated they heard a cry or moan. Without investigating, they hurried to the nearest blockhouse for safety. Such quick action probably saved their lives.

William Moore returned that day from Fort Butler, which was near present-day St. Jacob in Madison County. When evening fell, William journeyed to his brother's cabin to inquire about his missing children. After being told that John and George had left with Rachel Reagan and had not been seen since, William and his wife, Polly, embarked on a frantic search, each taking a different path. When calling for the children, William stumbled over something in the darkness. To his horror, he discovered a child's body. Without even attempting to identify the corpse, he hurried back to Abel and Mary Moore's cabin to warn everyone that a band of marauding Indians was in the area. He urged them to take cover in the blockhouse on his farm. They insisted, however, on accompanying him as he left to find his wife.

Meanwhile, Polly had been riding her horse over the trail when she spotted someone who appeared to be asleep on the ground. Unable to recognize the person in the darkness, she began calling out the names of the missing children in an attempt to draw a response. Dismounting, she approached the figure and discovered the mutilated corpse of Rachel Reagan, her sister. Three-year-old Timothy, barely conscious and covered with blood, was lying next to his mother. The child stirred and gasped, "The black man raised his axe and cut them again." Polly quickly remounted her horse and rode to her cabin, where she heated a pot of water to boiling. She had no weapon to protect herself. If the Indians invaded her cabin, she was prepared to throw the boiling water at them as a desperate, last-ditch attempt at self-defense. Fortunately, she was soon discovered by her husband and the search party.

The terrified settlers spent an anxious night in the blockhouse of William Moore, waiting for the Indian attack they felt was imminent. Around 3:00 a.m., they sent John Harris, who lived with Abel and Mary Moore, to Fort Russell, which was a few miles northwest of present-day Edwardsville, to seek help. Nine men, under the command of Captain Samuel Whiteside, arrived at dawn and assisted the families in their search for the victims' bodies. Abel Moore returned to the settlement with them. A path linking the cabins of the Moores and Reagans terminated at the west fork of the Wood River. The bodies were discovered along this path. All had been tomahawked to death, scalped and stripped of their clothing. Timothy Reagan, who had spoken to Polly the night before, was still alive. In an address delivered before the Illinois State Lyceum on December 6, 1832, the Reverend Thomas Lippincott, a Madison County pioneer who knew Abel and Mary Moore, stated that the child "was sitting near its mother's corpse, alive, with a gash, deep and large, on each side of its little face." Timothy died later that day.

It was decided to bury the victims on some nearby land that the pioneers had been using as a graveyard. The bodies were hauled to their place of interment on rough sleds drawn by oxen. They were buried in three adjacent graves: one for Rachel Reagan and her children, the second for William and Joel and the third for John and George. Since there were no coffin makers among these settlers, the seven corpses were interred with boards laid beneath, beside and above their bodies. This pioneer graveyard is now Vaughn Hill Cemetery, located on Illinois Route 111, about midway between the cities of Bethalto and Wood River.

This monument to the victims of the Wood River Massacre was erected in 1910 and can be seen on Fosterburg Road, which is just outside of Alton.

Whiteside vowed to kill the murderers and set out in pursuit. Although a captain in the Territorial Rangers, Abel Moore was permitted to remain at the settlement to comfort his wife and bury their two children. The weather was hot, and the rangers' horses often gave out and fell beneath their riders. Two days after leaving the Wood River Settlement, Whiteside and the rangers caught up with the Indians in present-day Morgan County near a creek that empties into the Sangamon River. Some of the Kickapoos had climbed a cottonwood tree to keep watch.

When Whiteside's militia was spotted, the Indians scattered. Whiteside's men then split up to give pursuit. One militia member, James Pruitt (sometimes spelled Preuitt), wounded one of the Native Americans in the thigh from a distance of thirty feet. When the Indian took refuge at the top of a fallen tree, Pruitt's brother, Abraham, shot him. The warrior died before he was able to fire his musket at the Pruitts. Upon searching his shot pouch, the brothers discovered the scalp of Rachel Reagan. Of the ten Indians in the party, only one escaped death. According to Volney P. Richmond in "The Wood River Massacre: A Reliable and Trustworthy Account," which was published in the January 8, 1899 edition of the *Alton Evening Telegraph*, this stream henceforth became known as Indian Creek "in honor of the event." The creek bears that name to this day.

Although the victims of the Wood River Massacre had been avenged, the tragedy continued to have lethal repercussions. Later that year, a territorial law was enacted that provided a fifty-dollar reward for any Native American, dead or alive, who entered a pioneer settlement. The law further provided a bounty of one hundred dollars for any Native American man, woman or child taken prisoner or killed in Native American territory.

On September 11, 1910, the twenty-one grandchildren of Abel and Mary Moore who lived in southern Illinois formally dedicated a monument to Rachel Reagan and the six children. This twenty-foot monument, constructed of concrete, was placed on the trail that once linked the cabins of the Reagan and Moore families in the Wood River Settlement and can be viewed today on Fosterburg Road. It was erected under the supervision of Dr. Isaac Moore, the son of Civil War veteran Major Franklin Moore. Franklin Moore (1826–1905) was the youngest child of Abel and Mary Moore.

The event was well attended. The *Alton Evening Telegraph* reported, "The wagon road was choked with buggies and automobiles for a long distance in the neighborhood of the monument, and there were many who went on foot to attend the dedication." Another monument to the victims was erected in

Erected in 1980, this monument to the Wood River Massacre victims is located a short distance from the graves of Abel and Mary Moore.

1980 on Illinois Route 140 and stands just one hundred yards from the grave site of Abel and Mary Moore.

For some years, there has been a poignant memorial to the massacre victims in the Alton Museum of History and Art: the original tombstone for Joel and William, which was hand carved by their bereaved father. The inscription reads: "William & Joel Moore were killed by the Indians July 10, 1814." According to an article published in the spring 2007 edition of the Alton Museum of History and Art's newsletter, the stone was removed from the Vaughn Hill Cemetery by the Moore family at some undetermined point in the past when the Moores discovered that the boys' grave was not being properly maintained. The family then donated the stone to a museum in Springfield, where it was either lost or discarded.

Brenda Kelley of Riverton, Illinois, found the grave marker on July 10, 1979—the 165th anniversary of the massacre—in her backyard while digging out shrubs. She believed the stone might have been in dirt that had been hauled by a previous owner to fill the yard. The marker was returned to southern Illinois, where the Alton Museum of History and Art, the Wood River Heritage Council and the City Cemetery Commission of Wood River all recognize its unique historical importance.

On March 26, 2007, local resident Kay Stobbs Massey donated to the Alton Museum of History and Art the original tombstone for John and George. Massey's parents discovered the tombstone in their home in the 1970s. It had been placed on top of the limestone foundation wall. Unfortunately, it is only a portion of the grave marker, and much of the inscription is missing. The capital letters appear to read:

JOHN
GEORGE
KILED [*sic*] BY INDIANS
JULY THE

While both tombstones certainly possess historical significance, this writer prefers visiting Rattan's Prairie to see the original grave marker for Abel and Mary Moore. Not on display in any museum, it still rests where it was placed in 1846 by the grieving children of this pioneer couple. In addition to marking their grave and the site of their first cabin, this primitive tombstone also serves to commemorate the long-vanished Wood River Settlement and the courageous pioneers who carved it out of the wilderness.

THE MYSTERY OF JEAN LAFITTE'S GRAVE

Pirates are traditionally associated with the high seas, particularly the Caribbean. Nonetheless, pirates also plied their nefarious trade on inland waters—including the Mississippi River where it flows past southwestern Illinois. Their activities were by no means confined to the Prairie State's pioneer era, and unlike the popular stereotype of pirates, they didn't limit their booty to gold and silver.

The October 17, 1901 edition of the *Alton Evening Telegraph* carried an account of "a daring robbery" at the city's Boston Store, which was a clothing store located near the river. "A gang of river pirates, probably part of a gang that has been plundering stores and towns up the river last year, dropped into Alton, and after picking up two boatloads of clothing went on their way," the article reads.

A police officer spotted the robbers in the store but mistook them for clerks. Later, however, a local resident noticed that the door had been broken open and part of the door's glass had been broken out. He summoned the police. The store owner soon arrived as well and discovered that "210 suits of boys' and men's clothing" had been stolen, along with "shoes, ladies silk waists and many other articles of apparel."

While these river pirates bear little resemblance to the swashbuckling pirates of yore, southwestern Illinois has a surprising connection to a pirate of almost mythic proportions: the legendary Jean Lafitte.

Separating fact from fiction is no easy task when writing about Jean Lafitte. In March 1813, when he applied to the French consul in New Orleans for a privateer's license, he gave his age as thirty-two and named Bordeaux, France, as his birthplace. Some historians believe Lafitte may have been born in Bayonne, France, or on the West Indies island of St. Dominique. While France may have recognized Lafitte and his older brother, Pierre, as privateers, the British and Spanish whose ships they preyed on regarded the two as pirates. American authorities generally shared that opinion.

Although Lafitte sought a formal license to engage in privateering in 1813, he and Pierre appear to have begun preying on ships in the Gulf of Mexico at least a decade earlier. The brothers established their base of operations in the swamps and bayous of Louisiana's Barataria Bay. Jean ruled the "Kingdom of Barataria," as the pirates' colony came to be called, as though it were an autonomous state. Lafitte's men captured scores of Spanish vessels, many of which carried slaves. These pirates converted their booty into cash by holding auctions in the swamps near New Orleans that drew bidders from the business community of the Crescent City. To protect his pirate kingdom, Lafitte began to store vast quantities of gunpowder and cannonballs, an arsenal that would play a critical role in the Battle of New Orleans.

The United States had entered the War of 1812 with high expectations. Britain was locked in a bitter conflict with Napoleonic France, which made it seem quite vulnerable to Congress's young war hawks such as Henry Clay and John C. Calhoun. Even a respected intellectual like former president Thomas Jefferson thought that conquering Canada would be "a mere matter of marching." The possibility of dramatically expanding American borders, in conjunction with repeated incidents of the British navy stopping American ships on the high seas to seize cargo it deemed contraband and pressing American sailors into British service, played a vital role in goading President James Madison and Congress to declare war on Britain.

Even while waging war against Napoleon, however, Britain proved to be a formidable foe for the young United States. France's defeat in 1814 allowed Britain to concentrate its forces on its former colony. America's most humiliating defeat occurred in August of that year when the American militia at Bladensburg, Maryland, was soundly defeated, allowing the British to advance on the nation's capital. President Madison fled to Virginia, while the British commanders feasted on the meal that had been prepared for the chief executive. The White House and U.S. Treasury were then burned.

The British tried to follow up this success by capturing the vital port of Baltimore but failed to force Fort McHenry to surrender, an American victory that inspired Francis Scott Key to pen "The Star-Spangled Banner." Still, the loss of our nation's capital proved devastating to American morale.

The war had never been popular in New England, where the Federalist Party continued to show strength. Gouverneur Morris, who had drafted the U.S. Constitution, openly called for New England and New York to secede from the Union, a proposal that a majority of Federalists came to support. The United States, barely a quarter of a century old, was in danger of dissolving. Only a dramatic military victory could defeat the British as well as those Americans who advocated secession.

Lafitte and the men of Barataria had remained neutral during the War of 1812. In late 1814, a British military delegation threatened to send a fleet to destroy Lafitte's pirate kingdom unless the Baratarians assisted the British in their campaign to capture New Orleans. When New Orleans was secured, the British army would move up the Mississippi and, acting in concert with British forces in Canada, utterly rout all American resistance.

The terms of the deal were enticing. If Lafitte threw in with the British, he and his Baratarians would receive full pardons for privateering as well as land within the British territory of North America. His majesty's army would free Pierre Lafitte, who was imprisoned in New Orleans and faced hanging for piracy. To sweeten the deal even further, the British offered Jean Lafitte £30,000—more than $2 million in today's money—if he and the Baratarians fought the Americans.

Lafitte told the delegation that he accepted the offer but needed two weeks to prepare his men for the campaign. He then contacted the Louisiana government and revealed the British plan. Despite the tempting offer, Lafitte's loyalty belonged to his adopted homeland.

Pierre shortly escaped or bribed his way out of jail and rejoined his brother, but the pirates were disconcerted to learn that the Americans intended to repay Jean Lafitte for conveying such vital information by sending a force to destroy Barataria. Lafitte gave strict orders to offer no resistance. The Americans attacked on September 16, 1814, and the pirates fled into the swamp, leaving behind about $600,000 of stolen goods as well as their cannon-laden ships. The community's buildings were put to the torch, and the Kingdom of Barataria was wiped from the face of the earth.

General Andrew Jackson arrived in New Orleans in November 1814 to take command of the American forces. Recognizing the need to shore up the city's defense, Jackson met with Lafitte and decided to enlist his support. Jackson had commandeered many of Lafitte's cannons but was

The subject of this painting, by an unknown artist, is thought to be Jean Lafitte. *Courtesy of Rosenberg Library, Galveston, Texas.*

The Battle of New Orleans, in which Jean Lafitte played a decisive role. *Public domain, Wikipedia Commons.*

woefully short of gunpowder and cannonballs. Lafitte, on the other hand, had a plethora of both stashed in the nearby swamps. The Baratarians, as experienced privateers, were excellent artillerymen who could lob these cannonballs with uncanny accuracy at the British.

The Battle of New Orleans, which raged through late December 1814 to mid-January 1815, was a stunning victory for the United States. The long rifles of Jackson's Tennessee and Kentucky marksmen combined with artillery batteries staffed by Lafitte's men decimated the British. Although the New Orleans victory actually occurred after the Americans and British had signed the Treaty of Ghent that formally ended the War of 1812, Jackson and Lafitte's triumph had profound consequences. Great Britain now respected the United States as a formidable power. The status of the young giant of the West had risen dramatically in the eyes of the world.

The victory had an equally momentous effect within American borders. Members of the Federalist Party from five states had held a convention in Hartford, Connecticut, in December 1814 and passed resolutions supporting the right of states to divert federal tax revenue for state defense and to shield citizens from military conscription. A delegation taking these resolutions to President Madison was preceded by news of the New Orleans victory.

The Federalists were now tainted in the eyes of most Americans as a clique of defeatists and secessionists. Voters abandoned the party in droves. Its presidential candidate in 1816 carried just three states. The Federalist Party—the party of John Adams and Alexander Hamilton—was finished in national politics.

President Madison issued a pardon for Lafitte and the Baratarians as a reward for their role in the Battle of New Orleans. Lafitte was free to begin a new life as a law-abiding citizen. After reacquiring at auction the stolen property and armed ships that had been seized during the raid on Barataria, however, he departed New Orleans and obtained a privateering license from the marque of Cartagena, a Colombian seaport.

Lafitte established a new pirate kingdom known as Campeche at Galveston, Texas, and resumed plundering ships in Gulf waters. By 1818, unscrupulous merchants from as far away as St. Louis were purchasing merchandise that had been stolen by Lafitte's band. When Campeche was destroyed by a hurricane, Lafitte and his men rebuilt their pirate community. Lafitte survived the wrath of nature. Surviving the wrath of a president proved considerably more challenging.

President James Monroe was angered that the man pardoned by his predecessor for heroic service during the Battle of New Orleans had returned to his old trade. His anger turned to outrage in 1820 when one of Lafitte's men plundered an American vessel. Lafitte attempted to placate Monroe by hanging the miscreant, but the chief executive sent a war brig to Campeche. The captain issued an ultimatum to Lafitte and his pirates: vacate Campeche or face expulsion by U.S. armed forces. After stalling for time, Lafitte finally complied in 1821.

Now the story gets complicated.

After leaving Campeche, Lafitte is said to have established a third pirate kingdom on Mugeres Island, which is located off the coast of Yucatan. It failed to flourish, however, and the great Jean Lafitte was reduced to piracy pure and simple when he could not obtain a privateer's license. Herbert Asbury, in *The French Quarter: An Informal History of the New Orleans Underworld*, stated that Lafitte entered the Indian village of Teljas, on the mainland, in 1826, where he died of a fever. The Lafitte Society of Galveston, Texas, noted that Lafitte disappeared after escaping from prison in Puerto Principe, Cuba, in February 1822. There are no confirmed sightings of Lafitte after the early 1820s, while reports of his death in a sea battle in the Gulf of Honduras in 1823 are not confirmed by primary sources.

And now the story gets really complicated.

In 1952, Stanley Clisby Arthur published *Jean Laffite, Gentleman Rover*, a biography that drew on material provided by one John Andrechyne Lafflin of Kansas City, Missouri, who claimed to be the great-grandson of the privateer-private. Lafflin, who argued that his famous ancestor's name should be spelled with two Fs, possessed what he maintained were his great-grandfather's journal as well as a family Bible that detailed Lafitte's life after vanishing from history in the early 1820s. The journal was discovered in an old trunk owned by the family, Lafflin said. Arthur, grateful for the historical material that Lafflin provided, dedicated the book to him.

Lafflin, who is now deceased, had Lafitte's journal published by Vantage Press, a vanity press firm, in 1958. The original journal, as well as the family Bible, are on display at the Sam Houston Regional Library and Research Center in Liberty, Texas.

The journal has Lafitte born on April 22, 1782, at Port-au-Prince, Haiti, the son of a French father and a mother who was a Sephardic Jew. His maternal grandfather, according to this account, was persecuted by the Inquisition and died of starvation in a Spanish prison. Jean and Pierre were educated at schools on Martinique and St. Croix. It was on the latter island, Lafitte's alleged journal tells us, where they took a course in psychology so they could gain a better understanding of human nature. The reader is left to surmise to what extent a knowledge of psychology, which did not exist as an academic discipline until the late nineteenth century, aided Lafitte during his career as a privateer and pirate.

Young Jean affirmed his Jewish heritage by marrying Christine Levine, a Danish Jew who lived in the Virgin Islands and bore the pirate three children before dying of fever. He married twenty-three-year-old Emma Hortense Mortimore at Charleston, South Carolina, in 1832, a union recorded in the family Bible owned by Lafflin. Lafitte fathered two sons by his second wife: one who died at age twelve and Jules, who lived to carry on the ancestral line.

The retired pirate changed his name to Lafflin in an effort to escape his past and establish a new life. He moved to St. Louis, where he founded a gunpowder business known as Lafflin, Lafflin and Smith. The gentleman rover took time away from work to travel to Europe in 1847, according to a journal entry, where he met such celebrities as Alexis de Tocqueville, Louis Braille, Louis Daguerre and even Karl Marx and Friedrich Engels. Arthur reproduced a two-page letter in *Gentleman Rover* that Lafitte supposedly wrote from Brussels in which the pirate stated that he intended to finance Marx's activities but refused an invitation to help compose *The Communist Manifesto*. In another letter reproduced in *Gentleman Rover*, Lafitte states his intention to introduce Marx's writings to a promising young Illinois politician named Abraham Lincoln.

After the death of his son, the family of three moved to southwestern Illinois. Lafitte evidently was already familiar with the East Side. His journal bears dated entries when he visited such towns as Belleville, Carlinville,

Edwardsville and Bethalto. The Bethalto references is especially intriguing, since it is dated May 4, 1846. It is a matter of historical record that the community now known as Bethalto was not called by that name until the mid-1850s.

According to Arthur, the adventurer whose name once struck terror in the hearts of merchant ship crews in Gulf waters perished because of a good deed. Lafitte learned that an aged, indigent friend and his wife, who lived on a farm outside of Edwardsville, were hungry and ill. He journeyed in the rain to their home and discovered them cold as well. Always the good Samaritan, Lafitte chopped some wood for the couple, thus getting even wetter. He came down with pneumonia the next day and died in Alton on May 5, 1854, at age seventy-seven.

Jules and Emma both wrote entries in the family Bible to note Lafitte's death. Following a Mass, Lafitte was supposedly buried in the northwest section of a Catholic cemetery located about a mile north of Alton. Jules and his mother left Alton that summer, never to return. Emma, according to this account, never remarried and died in Philadelphia in 1885.

Lafitte's alleged journal is written in French, a language that John Lafflin, a railroad engineer, claimed he didn't know. The Vantage Press edition of the journal contains a letter from David C. Mearns, chief of the Manuscript Division at the Library of Congress, attesting that the paper on which the journal is written appears to be from the early nineteenth century.

John Lafflin claimed in 1958 that his grandfather took him to visit the pirate's grave in 1922. Don Huber, former Alton township supervisor and local historian, has affirmed that a Catholic cemetery indeed once existed at the present-day 700 block of Northdale Drive in Alton, adjacent to the Confederate Cemetery. Known simply as the "Old Catholic Cemetery," it was used for burials only from 1848 to 1858. The cemetery records were destroyed years ago in a fire, however. The site is now heavily wooded, and the tombstones were carried off over the years by vandals.

Arthur's biography as well as the journal and family Bible on which he drew for the controversial biography have won more than a few converts to the view that Lafitte is buried in Alton. A doctoral candidate in education at the University of Illinois, while vacationing with his wife in the bayou country near New Orleans in the early 1960s, was astounded when their guide concluded his account of Lafitte by noting that he was buried in the southwestern Illinois city. Alfred Leavell Jr. utilized Arthur's book and the alleged journal when writing his 1966 master's thesis about early Alton history at Southern Illinois University at Edwardsville.

Alan Harrison, a member of the Sons of the American Revolution, made a presentation in 2000 to Alton Museum of History and Art board members and several city officials in which he stated that he believed Lafitte might well be buried in Alton. Harrison examined entries in Lafitte's journal against old St. Louis City Directories and other sources. The rate of correlation was quite good, and he concluded that the journal was authentic.

Reputable historians have long declared Lafitte's journal a fraud, however. Charles Van Ravenswaay, director of the Missouri Historical Society, denounced the journal in a 1953 letter to Alton High School history teacher Don Lewis. Van Ravenswaay argued that there was no proof of Lafitte's residence in St. Louis or his supposed ownership of a gunpowder business.

Arthur's biography includes a photograph of an alleged Manuel de Franca painting of Lafitte, his second wife and their two sons that was said to be done in St. Louis around 1842. The original painting, according to the caption, hangs in Lafflin's home. Van Ravenswaay said that the painting did not correspond in style to de Franca paintings in the collection of the Missouri State Historical Society. He also maintained that the clothing worn by the people in the painting was historically inaccurate for the 1840s. Van Ravenswaay and Lewis, now both deceased, were convinced that the journal was a fraud. Arthur's Lafitte biography was hopelessly flawed, they concluded, and Jean Lafitte could not possibly be buried in Alton.

Still, no amount of academic skepticism likely will ever discourage the true believers. Visitors to Alton have been known to stop by the author's bookshop to ask for directions to "the cemetery where Jean Lafitte is buried." Rumors still abound that Lafitte might have buried some of his pirate's loot in the area, although—thankfully—no excavations have been attempted. Lafitte undoubtedly would be pleased to know that his mystique has continued into the twenty-first century.

AN ABUSED SLAVE AND
THE WOMAN WHO SAVED HIM

Modern readers might find it amusing that the *Alton Evening Telegraph*, which was founded in 1836, was running a feature titled "Talks with the Old Settlers" in the 1870s. However, the newspaper's editorial department astutely realized that the members of the pioneer generation were rapidly dying off and their stories must be preserved before they were forever lost.

On New Year's Eve of 1874, the newspaper carried an astonishing account of a slave's abuse at the hands of a local racist. The narrative was written by Dr. George T. Allen, who identified himself as a surgeon at the Marine Hospital of St. Louis, Missouri. Opened in 1850, the Marine Hospital in Allen's day stood at 3640 Marine Avenue in St. Louis. The institution no longer exists. Allen died just two years after this account appeared in Alton's newspaper.

Allen and his parents arrived in Edwardsville on December 23, 1817, after making a journey of "more than three months" from New York. The Allen family was accompanied by "a Negro boy, named Henry, aged 18 years, and a Negro girl named Jane, 8 years old, both given to my mother by her father." Allen recalled that Henry cried bitterly on Christmas Eve because "he wasn't in Old Master's kitchen in New York to fill himself with cider and apples and New Year's cakes and ginger bread." To learn more about the treatment of slaves during the holiday season, consult my 2010 book for Arcadia/The History Press *From Christmas to Twelfth Night in Southern Illinois*.

Although New Yorkers, the Allens were well familiar with slavery. According to the New York Historical Society, the Empire State in 1799 passed a Gradual Emancipation Act that freed slave children born after July 4, 1799, but indentured them until adulthood. Another law, passed in 1817, freed those born into slavery before 1799 but not until 1827. The 1830 census revealed that there were only seventy-five slaves in the entire state. The 1840 census indicated that no slaves lived in New York City.

Although the Northwest Ordinance of 1787 forbade the introduction of slavery into Illinois, the peculiar institution existed in the Prairie State under the guise of indentured servitude. Indeed, the first four governors of Illinois held slaves. For more information about slavery in the state, read my 2011 book for Arcadia/The History Press, *Abolitionism and the Civil War in Southwestern Illinois*.

In addition to settlers from the northeastern states such as the Allens, southwestern Illinois also drew pioneers from Dixie, and these southerners brought their proslavery sentiments with them. When these transplanted southerners encountered antislavery Illinoisans, violence frequently ensued. Allen's account in the *Alton Evening Telegraph* chronicles a particularly horrifying incident.

James Henry, a transplanted Kentuckian and "a very bitter pro-slavery man," was in Edwardsville on "one of his quarterly sprees" when he decided that Jarret, a slave owned by a lawyer named Conway, had insulted him. Henry demanded that Conway allow him to avenge this slight to his honor, and "Conway's cowardice led him to grant the favor."

When Jarret learned of his impending fate, he fled to the stable of Allen's father and hid in the hay. "I knew this," Allen wrote, "and secretly fed and watered the poor negro." Unfortunately, a "drunken hostler" revealed Jarret's hiding place to Henry. Allen's memoir then succinctly provides this proslavery man's preparation for the ensuing horrors:

> *Jim Henry then provided himself with five hickory whips, fresh from the timber, a rope, his sword, his dagger—a regular bowie knife—and a pistol. He then sought and found Jarret, tied him, brought him out, stripped him of all clothing excepting his pants, and fastened him to the end of a horse-rack, on the public street, so as to compel him to stand on his toes. Henry laid his sword and pistol on the horse-block some three feet from his victim, and with the dagger in his left hand and a hickory in his right, commenced the castigation.*

Henry's abuse of Jarret quickly drew a crowd. "It was 'Court week' in Edwardsville," Allen wrote, "and there seemed to me—a little boy then—five

Edwardsville, where this incident occurred, is named after Ninian Edwards, who served as the territorial governor of Illinois, U.S. senator from Illinois and the third governor of Illinois.

hundred men in town and all present and looking on!" The transplanted Kentuckian "wore out two or three—I think three—hickory gads on Jarret's bare back. With nearly every blow the blood ran." Jarret occasionally pulled himself up on the rope and begged for mercy. This sadist possessed no mercy, however. "The white brute," as Allen called him, "would draw the keen edge of his immense knife over the prisoner's naked abdomen and threaten to let out his bowels if he failed to stand."

Allen recalled that Henry "dared any man to interfere and intimidated the Sheriff and constables and all the men present, with his sword, his dagger and his pistol." He then wrote a few short lines that revealed Henry had little reason to fear interference by the gawkers. "In that day and that community, no sympathy was felt for the 'nigger' [Allen's quotation marks]. If the man had been white, Henry would not have struck him the second blow and lived. The negro then had no rights the white man even pretended to regard."

No man present even attempted to rescue Jarret. A courageous woman—Sarah Townsend Allen, the mother of the memoir's author—performed that task.

> *Just when the second or third whip had been used up, my mother first heard the poor negro's cry and she went immediately to his rescue. She appealed to all the men present, but unheeded. Then she retired to her kitchen, armed herself with a formidable carving knife and immediately advanced upon the enemy. Henry did not see her until she had nearly touched the negro; when he suspended his blow, in astonishment, but with still a threatening gesture. She raised the knife, cut the rope and ordered the sufferer into her own kitchen, where she dressed his wounds most carefully, with her own hands.*

Henry made no attempt to stop her rescue of Jarret. Perhaps he couldn't bring himself to assault a white woman. Evidently trying to save face from what he regarded as a defeat, he turned to the crowd, waved his dagger and said, "A woman might tie my hands, but let a man thus try to oppose my will." This concluded that portion of Allen's memoir that dealt with Jarret's ordeal.

Sarah Allen's rescue of Jarret is even more remarkable in light of the fact that, as her son pointed out, she was a slaveholder and had brought her two captives to Illinois. Unlike many other slaveholders, Sarah Allen possessed a conscience and found Henry's torture of Jarret intolerable.

Beverly Bauser, who researched this long-ago horror, wrote that Sarah Townsend Allen died on October 7, 1846, at age fifty-seven. She, her husband and George T. Allen are all buried in the Marine Cemetery in St. Jacobs, Illinois. "I could find no further information on James Henry or Jarret," she wrote. We can only hope that Jarret lived long enough to be freed from slavery.

THE FIRST DUEL IN ILLINOIS

Around 1800, a sandbar appeared in the Mississippi River near the present site of East St. Louis, Illinois. Soil deposits grew this sandbar to an island about a mile long and five hundred feet wide. It never had any residents but occasionally hosted some deadly visitors.

Regarded as politically neutral since it belonged to neither Illinois nor Missouri, this small island served as a field of honor for aggrieved Missourians who wanted to duel without facing legal consequences. The number of duels fought on this patch of land gave it the name Bloody Island. Thanks to the engineering skills of a young U.S. Army officer named Robert E. Lee who came to St. Louis to improve river navigation, Bloody Island eventually merged with the Illinois riverfront.

The duelists who drew blood on Bloody Island during its brief existence were prominent Missourians such as Thomas Hart Benton, who engaged in two duels on Bloody Island in 1817—both with the same man. The future U.S. senator and his opponent, an attorney named Charles Lucas, wounded each other during their first duel. Benton shot Lucas dead during their second encounter.

While such episodes make for colorful narrative, they belong to the realm of Missouri history. Although Illinois had no counterpart to Bloody Island, dueling was not unknown. In fact, the first known duel in the Prairie State occurred in the southwestern Illinois city of Belleville on February 8, 1819.

According to an account of this duel written by one James Afflect, who identified himself as "a citizen of Belleville at the time of its occurrence,"

Missouri lawyer and politician Thomas Hart Benton, who killed his opponent in a duel on Bloody Island. *National Portrait Gallery, Washington, D.C. Wikipedia Commons.*

the dispute between the two participants arose from "a very trivial matter." Afflect's narrative, which was published in *Transactions of the Illinois State Historical Society for the Year 1901*, identified the duelists as Alfonso C. Stuart and Timothy Bennett. Stuart, we are told, "was an educated man, from the state of New York, and a lawyer by profession, but unfortunately, his practice was more frequent at Tannehill's bar than that of Judge Reynolds." John Reynolds, whose law office was located in nearby Cahokia, was elected an associate justice of the Illinois Supreme Court by the legislature in 1818. Afflect's narrative informs us "Stuart and Bennett were both young men in the prime of life, each having a family."

It seems that Bennett's horse repeatedly entered Stuart's cornfield, "which greatly enraged the latter, and he told Bennett if he didn't keep his horse out of his field he would shoot the horse." When the horse trespassed yet again, Stuart instructed his hired man to shoot the animal with a muzzle-loading firearm of that era that had been "loaded with powder and coarse salt." The horse, which was one of Bennett's favorites, ran home bleeding.

Bennett "became greatly enraged over the shooting of his horse" by Stuart's man and sought revenge. It was Bennett's misfortune to possess such feelings when he encountered Jacob Short and Nathaniel Fike, two men characterized by Afflect as "a pair of young Bacchanalians"—rowdies who were given to excessive alcohol consumption. Appropriately enough, Bennett ran into Short and Fike where they "made their haunt, and hibernated, at Tannehill's tavern, which then occupied the southwest corner of the public square on Main Street, the site of the present National Hotel."

Short and Fike decided to have some amusement at Bennett's expense. They convinced him that Stuart "had grievously injured and insulted him" and he should challenge the man who had ordered his favorite horse shot to a duel. Bennett agreed. Later, however, Short and Fike saw Stuart and told him it was to be "a sham duel." They would act as seconds and make sure the weapons would be loaded with only powder. The entire affair "was only intended to enliven the monotony of life in the then small village," according to Afflect. But this practical joke soon turned deadly.

The parties made arrangements for the duel at the county courthouse, which was "then located on the southwest corner of Main and Illinois streets, in front of James Tannehill's tavern, with whom the writer was then living." News of the impending duel quickly spread throughout the community. Young men teased Bennett "by telling him that he would take the 'Duck ague' and couldn't shoot with accuracy." Duck ague, also known as "buck ague" or "buck fever," refers to a hunter who takes aim at an animal but suddenly loses his nerve and misses the shot. Bennett was not amused. He silenced his detractors by loading his rifle and shooting off the head of a chicken in a nearby yard.

The four men "were pretty full of Tannehill's whiskey" when they entered the dueling ground, which "was located about midway between Main street and the present mansion of the late Adam W. Snyder." Stuart and Bennett stood about twenty-five steps apart when the order to "Fire!" was spoken.

Afflect wrote that "Bennett fired and Stuart fell, face downward, to the ground shot in the region of the heart. He fell on his gun and immediately expired." Contrary to what Short and Fike had told Stuart, Bennett's weapons had not been loaded with just powder. Afflect wrote that Stuart "was buried about a hundred yards from where he fell, northwest."

Fike, who had served as Stuart's second, took the dead man's rifle "and discharged it in the air, so that it was never known whether it contained a ball or not" although "there was a suspicion with many that the crack of the gun was that of one containing a ball." Bennett, Short and Fike were arrested and jailed. Short and Fike were soon released on bail, however, while Bennett remained incarcerated.

This duel occurred at an awkward time in Illinois history. The Prairie State had been admitted into the Union just a year earlier, and according to Afflect, Illinois "had neither law, nor officials, to try prisoners in St. Clair county." The state legislature rose to the occasion, however, and "proceeded at once to enact laws for the emergency, and to appoint officials." A special court was set up, and Bennett, Short and Fike were all indicted for Stuart's murder.

Bennett evidently believed that a guilty verdict was a foregone conclusion and escaped from the log jail on the eve of his trial. He fled to "the wilds of the Arkansas Territory," where his precise whereabouts remained unknown for two and a half years. It was then learned—Afflect doesn't record how and by whom—that Bennett was living in the old French village of Ste. Genevieve, Missouri. He had managed to contact his wife—again, Afflect doesn't say how—and expressed his desire to see her and their children.

Since returning to Belleville was out of the question, Bennett sent a team and wagon for her and the children.

As a solitary fugitive in "the wilds of the Arkansas Territory," Bennett had been untraceable. His desire to see his loved ones again, however, proved to be his undoing. James Tannehill, the owner of the tavern where the principals involved in this affair had liquored up before the duel, organized a posse that followed Bennett's family on their journey. Why? According to Afflect, there was a reward for his capture. Afflect and his men arrested Bennett and brought him back to Belleville to stand trial.

The judicial deck was stacked against Bennett. Short and Fike had been tried after Bennett's escape. Both were acquitted "by the testimony of Rachael Tannehill, a girl of nine or ten years, who was looking out of an upper window in the Tannehill tavern at the time the party was starting for the duelling ground." This child claimed that she saw Bennett "come around the court house" and "saw him put something into his gun which the jury construed to be a bullet." Her testimony persuaded the jury that Bennett himself had loaded his firearm with the lead ball that killed Stuart.

Bennett was indeed convicted and sentenced to death by hanging. Afflect recalled that the execution, which took place on September 3, 1821, drew "one of the largest assemblages ever brought together in this county." To the end, Bennett insisted that he had not placed the fatal round in his weapon. Ironically, Bennett's defense lawyer was an attorney from Missouri, Thomas Hart Benton, who in 1817 had killed Charles Lucas in a duel on Bloody Island.

TICKETS TO A BLACK ABOLITIONIST'S HANGING

When I saw Paul Schneider's *Old Man River: The Mississippi River in North American History* in my hometown library's nonfiction section, I immediately decided to check it out. While the book contains much fascinating material, an advertising poster dated July 7, 1841, on page 260 should be particularly meaningful for area residents. The poster features a drawing of the *Eagle*, a well-known steamer packet, and announces that W.A. Wentworth and P.M. Pinckard have chartered the vessel "for the purpose of accommodating all the citizens of ALTON, and the vicinity, who may wish to see the Four Negroes Executed at St. Louis, on FRIDAY NEXT."

The *Eagle* would depart Alton at 7:00 a.m. and leave St. Louis about 4:00 p.m. "so as to reach home the same evening." The poster assures the public that "the Boat will be repaired and fitted up for the occasion; and every attention will be paid to the comfort of Passengers." Large bold letters followed by three exclamation points proclaim that this round-trip would cost only $1.50 per person. "The Negroes are to be hung on Duncan's Island, just below St. Louis," the poster continues. Since Duncan's Island would undoubtedly be crowded with spectators, the poster's final sentence reassures prospective customers that their view of the grim proceedings will be unobstructed. "The Boat will drop alongside, so that ALL CAN SEE WITHOUT DIFFICULTY."

There are no surviving receipts from this commercial venture, so we don't know how many area residents availed themselves of the opportunity to see the hanging of these four men. I found it interesting that the men, although

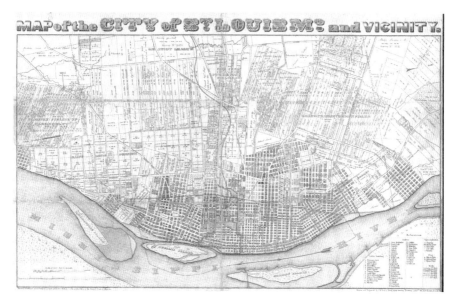

Mississippi River map. Duncan's Island, where the four men were hanged, is on the left. Bloody Island, a popular place for duels, is to the right. *Missouri History Museum*.

tried, convicted and sentenced to die in a court of law, were identified as "negroes" rather than "prisoners" or "condemned men." Perhaps Wentworth and Pinckard knew that the hanging of African Americans held a special attraction for area residents.

Indeed, the Illinois and Missouri racists who gleefully watched this execution took particular delight in seeing Charles Brown die. He wasn't just another Black man. Brown was an abolitionist, who, as an agent employed by the Ohio Anti-Slavery Society, had helped well over one hundred enslaved men and women attain freedom.

A.B. Chambers, editor and co-owner of the St. Louis–based *Missouri Republican* newspaper, transcribed autobiographical statements from Brown and the other three men following their convictions. Shortly before their execution, Chambers used his newspaper's printing press to publish a book titled *Trials and Confessions of Madison Henderson, alias Blanchard, Alfred Amos Warwick, James W. Seward and Charles Brown, Murderers of Jesse Baker and Jacob Weaver, as Given by Themselves; and a Likeness pf Each, Taken in Jail Shortly after Their Arrest*. In order to gain access to the condemned men, Chambers agreed to give George H.C. Melody, their jailer, co-authorship of the book—as well as a share of its profit. According to historian Thomas C. Buchanan, "The book was a considerable publishing success." It was especially popular among slavery apologists for supposedly proving the dangers of the abolitionist movement as well as free Black activism.

Born of free parents in South Carolina in 1814 or 1815, Charles Brown became acquainted with some abolitionists in Charleston and eventually made his way to Ohio's Oberlin College, where he remained for just two months. It was at Oberlin, the first American college to admit Black students, that Brown "acquired most of the limited education I have," he is quoted as saying in Chambers's book.

Brown's statement provides a fascinating glimpse into the workings of an antislavery society and its field activists. Agents, he told Chambers, were required to keep a record of those slaves they helped liberate and report these numbers to the society. Brown and other agents carried with them forged certificates of freedom that facilitated slaves' escape. Agents always encouraged slaves to take some of their master's money or property with them, Brown stated. This wasn't stealing, he and his fellow agents told the slaves, since they had assisted their masters in acquiring this wealth. "If the slave has no place he can secrete himself in the interior of the states," Brown remarked, "he is usually sent directly to Canada, where he is beyond his master's power to take him."

Brown liberated his first slave in New Orleans. Supplied by Brown with a certificate of freedom, the fugitive traveled by boat to Cincinnati and then took a stagecoach to Canada. Brown's starting salary with the Ohio Anti-Slavery Society was just thirty dollars per month, but it was soon raised to fifty per month because of his rate of success. As a free Black man who could ride steamboats, Brown had ready access to river cities. He estimated that he liberated about eighty slaves in the New Orleans area and sixteen in the vicinity of Vicksburg. "Besides these I supplied a great many with certificates and advised them how to get off," Brown recalled, "but in most cases I never knew whether they succeeded in getting away or not." He worked relentlessly in New Orleans and noted that, when he last left the city, "I had a list of about 60 whom I had promised to get off this spring or summer."

Unfortunately, Brown began supplementing his salary by stealing. He eventually joined a gang of criminals that preyed on the citizens of river cities. In April 1841, Jesse Baker and Jacob Weaver were murdered when this gang robbed a bank located on Water Street in St. Louis. Brown admitted in his statement to bludgeoning both men with a crowbar. He concluded by addressing his wife and newborn child with the hope that "God grant that we may all meet where there is no more trouble or death."

According to historian Mary E. Seematter, over twenty thousand spectators watched the execution from boats of every description and the St. Louis shore as well as on Duncan's Island itself. Brown's noose was loosely tied, and the crowd enjoyed the spectacle of the hated abolitionist suffering a slow, agonizing death from strangulation. The severed heads of the four men were prominently displayed in the window of Corse's Drug Store in St. Louis as a warning to those African Americans who might be tempted to commit murder or liberate slaves, which proslavery white men regarded as theft of private property.

Brown's confessed criminal activity and execution for murder profoundly embarrassed abolitionists and forever overshadowed his accomplishments in the antislavery movement. Personally, I like to think that some of the Alton area residents who paid $1.50 to watch Brown hanged eventually experienced a change of heart and made a matching donation to an antislavery society.

THE LINCOLN-SHIELDS DUEL

Americans revere Abraham Lincoln as our sixteenth president, who led our nation through the turmoil of the Civil War. Southwestern Illinois residents associate Lincoln with two events that occurred in this area: his final debate with Stephen A. Douglas in the 1858 senatorial campaign, which comprises a chapter in my book *Abolitionism and the Civil War in Southwestern Illinois*, and a duel Lincoln almost fought with Illinois state auditor James Shields in 1842 on an island in the Mississippi.

Shields, a respected attorney as well as an officeholder, issued a proclamation that year in conjunction with the governor and state treasurer. The proclamation directed the county tax collectors to refuse to honor the state's paper money as payment for taxes and school debts. Only gold and silver would be accepted—and the common people of Illinois had little of either. To make matters worse, Shields later issued a separate directive that attempted to advise state officers, the legislature and even the people on what he regarded as the best way to better their dire financial circumstances.

A loyal Democrat, Shields expected to incur the wrath of the Illinois Whigs by his actions, but a satiric personal attack in the press caught him by surprise. In August and September 1842, the *Sangamo Journal* of Springfield published four letters by a writer using the pseudonym "Rebecca" as well as a poem attributed to one "Cathleen." The works ridiculed Shields and even insinuated that he was guilty of misappropriating state funds. The Cathleen poem was especially malicious for deriding Shields for his birth in County Tyrone, Ireland. Scholars believe that the poem was written by Mary Todd.

James Shields was a proud man and quite sensitive about his Irish background. He sought out Simeon Francis, the editor of the newspaper, and demanded to know the author's identity. Francis capitulated and disclosed Rebecca's identity—Abraham Lincoln.

Shields was taken aback. He and Lincoln were old acquaintances who had served together in the legislature when Shields had won a seat in 1835. They had never been the best of friends, but there had been no animosity between them. Shields and Lincoln then embarked on a war of words, with the former demanding an apology and the latter—who admitted to writing at least one of the Rebecca letters—refusing to do so. Throwing caution to the wind, Shields finally challenged Lincoln to a duel, which the Great Commoner accepted.

As the challenged party, Lincoln set the terms of the duel. He informed Shields that the engagement would be fought with the largest type of cavalry broad swords within three miles of Alton on the opposite side of the river. Since dueling was illegal in Illinois, both parties knew that their confrontation must occur outside the state if they wanted to further their political careers.

The site of the duel was a small island opposite Alton that has been known by a number of names over the years, including the Towhead, Sunflower Island, Mosquito Island, McPike's Island and Willow Bug Island. Some accounts, however, have challenged this. An eyewitness to the duel stated many years later that Lincoln and Shields met not on any island but on Missouri soil, near a clearing owned by the Mahon family. But all accounts agree that the actual event more closely resembled comedy than any kind of deadly confrontation.

The two antagonists met on the appointed day of September 22, 1842. As they faced each other, according to one account, Lincoln demonstrated the tremendous advantage his six-feet, four-inch height gave him in a sword duel by cutting off a willow limb that hung high over the head of the much shorter Shields. The astute Hibernian realized the futility of his position and decided to end the matter before it had even begun. Another tale about the duel concerns the tense crowd that waited on the Alton levee for the victor to return from the island. Suddenly, the onlookers saw a boat making its way back to Alton with what appeared to be a bloody corpse lying near its bow. A number of women supposedly fainted.

The crowd surged forward to learn the identity of the fallen warrior, only to be flabbergasted when both Lincoln and Shields emerged from the boat and laughed at the crowd's credulity. The "corpse" was merely an old log that Lincoln had wrapped with a red shirt.

The Lincoln-Shields Recreation Area was named to commemorate the duel fought between Abraham Lincoln and James Shields on a Mississippi River island.

Upon disembarking, Lincoln and Shields purportedly retired to one of Alton's taverns and spent the rest of the day toasting each other's continued good health.

Shields's political career hardly suffered from the aborted duel. The ambitious state auditor later became the only person in American history to serve as a U.S. senator from three states: Illinois, Minnesota and Missouri. He also served his adopted country as a brigadier general during the Civil War. Shields's lifelong regret was that his Irish birth made him ineligible to seek the office that was eventually won by his opponent in the Alton duel.

In his later years, Lincoln found the duel episode an embarrassment. In a letter dated December 9, 1865, Mary Todd Lincoln recalled an army officer who visited the White House and asked her husband whether it was true that "you once went out, to fight a duel and all for the sake of the lady by your side?" According to his widow, Lincoln replied, "I do not deny it, but if you desire my friendship, you will never mention it again."

The island where the duel almost occurred is now known as the Lincoln-Shields Recreation Area. Some area residents, however, refer to it as Smallpox Island. How did it acquire such a menacing name? The answer is contained in my 2011 book published by Arcadia/The History Press: *Abolitionism and the Civil War in Southwestern Illinois*.

THE LYNCHING OF A SCHOOLTEACHER

According to Randall M. Miller in his article "Lynching in America," at least 3,500 lynchings occurred in our nation from 1865 to 1920, "mostly in the South during the period of black disenfranchisement and the enactment and initial implementation of Jim Crow laws." Later in his article, Miller quoted the assertion of historian W. Fitzhugh Brundage that lynching was so pervasive in the South it served "to define southern distinctiveness every bit as much as the Mason-Dixon line marked the boundary of the region."

While lynchings indeed occurred "mostly in the South," such murders also took place in other regions of the United States. Even many Illinoisans aren't aware that racially motivated lynchings have occurred in the Prairie State, which was the first state to ratify the Thirteenth Amendment after it was passed by Congress in 1865. A particularly horrifying lynching was perpetrated in Belleville on June 6, 1903.

David Wyatt held a master's degree from the University of Michigan and had embarked on a teaching career. He journeyed to Illinois and eventually settled in Brooklyn, a small community in St. Clair County. Founded by a band of freed and fugitive slaves, Brooklyn functioned as an important Underground Railroad station before the Civil War. For more information about this community, see my 2011 book *Abolitionism and the Civil War in Southwestern Illinois*.

In his book *America's First Black Town: Brooklyn, Illinois 1830–1915*, Sundiata Keita Cha-Jua stated that Black people in Brooklyn and throughout Illinois evidently held Wyatt in high esteem. He was active in the statewide Afro-American Teachers Association and in local Republican politics. Determined to eradicate illiteracy among adults, Wyatt started a night school for adults. Cha-Jua noted that Wyatt taught in the Brooklyn school district from 1893 until his death at the hands of a lynch mob.

Brooklyn, with its large Black majority, afforded Wyatt and its other residents a high degree of security. In Belleville, on the other hand, only five hundred of the city's seventeen thousand citizens were African American. The city's civil rights movement was in its infancy. Yet Wyatt was compelled to go to Belleville in order to be recertified to teach the following year.

On June 6, 1903, Wyatt pulled a revolver from his pocket and shot Charles Hertel, the St. Clair County superintendent of schools, while the two were inside Hertel's office, which was located in the county courthouse in Belleville. Cha-Jua speculated that Wyatt might have been carrying a revolver because he anticipated trouble. The two were known to have had a strained relationship. According to Dennis B. Downey's "A 'Many-Headed Monster': The 1903 Lynching of David Wyatt," the superintendent's past evaluations of Wyatt had been less than favorable. Matters came to a head that day when Hertel refused to recertify him, allegedly based on reports of Wyatt's cruelty toward his students.

George Fiedler, Hertel's assistant who was in the office that day, later told police that Wyatt had shouted at Hertel, "Then, damn you, you'll never sign another," which Downey believes was a reference to the teaching certificate that Hertel refused to sign. Wyatt was quickly subdued by two police officers. The sound of the gunshot drew a crowd that rapidly grew to as many as five hundred. Some members of the crowd called out "Lynch him!" and "Get a rope!" Eight policemen hastily escorted Wyatt from the courthouse to the jail, which was located four blocks away.

Wyatt was unknown to most residents of Belleville. When words spread that a white man had been shot by a Black man who was now incarcerated in the jail, however, a crowd estimated at five thousand quickly gathered outside the building. Downey quoted an account in the *St. Louis Post-Dispatch*, which observed that the crowd included "society ladies" riding in carriages as well as women who were "carrying their babies" or "leading small children." Some couples evidently treated this crisis as a social event. The *St. Louis Post-Dispatch* reporter also saw "well-dressed women, many of them leaning on the arms of escorts."

Fred J. Kern, Belleville's mayor, made a brief speech to the crowd in which he pleaded that the law be allowed to take its course. Crowd members responded by throwing rocks at Kern, who quickly retreated into the jail building. Downey wrote that the fire department turned its hose on the crowd in an effort to disperse it. Cha-Jua, however, stated the firemen unraveled their hose but couldn't bring themselves to unleash a high-pressure stream of water on their fellow townspeople. Crowd members made sure they would remain dry by cutting the fire hose into sections and then tying those sections into knots.

The Belleville police, whose officers had taken such determined measures to transport Wyatt from the courthouse to the jail, did nothing to thwart Wyatt's lynching. Their inaction wasn't motivated by apathy or racism, however. They were under specific orders to stand down. Since St. Clair County sheriff Wash Thompson was out of town, a triumvirate composed of Kern, St. Clair County state's attorney James Farmer and former judge M.W. Schaefer chose a course of action. The trio decided that police officers should not use force to deter those mob members who entered the jail to seize Wyatt. Kern was later quoted as saying that he ordered the police not to offer resistance because he didn't want any innocent blood shed. Wash Thompson later concurred with that fateful decision. The June 23, 1903 edition of the *St. Louis Republic* stated that Thompson "believes from the report the assistants made that they did the best they could to defend the jail without causing the loss of human life."

But a human life was lost that day. Perhaps Thompson didn't regard the life of David Wyatt as human.

Cha-Jua quoted a *St. Louis Post-Dispatch* account that stated the mob learned around 10:30 p.m. that the police were under orders to offer no resistance. Downey wrote that it was about 11:00 p.m. when a group of men and boys rushed the unattended rear door of the jail. It took mob members about thirty minutes to break open the lock of Wyatt's cell. When the doomed man was seized, a boy called out to the crowd, "We've got him." Crowd members cheered.

The account of Wyatt's lynching in the June 7, 1903 edition of the *New York Times* contained at least two factual errors in its opening sentence, which reads: "This has been the most exciting day Belleville has known in years, as the result of the lynching last night of David J. Wyatt, the East St. Louis school teacher, who fatally shot Charles Hertel, Superintendent of Schools in St. Clair County, at 6 o'clock Saturday evening."

Wyatt taught in Brooklyn, not in nearby East St. Louis. But such a minor error pales when compared to the unnamed journalist's statement that Wyatt "fatally shot" Hertel. The *Belleville News-Democrat* reported in its July 2, 1903 edition that Hertel "was out Thursday for the first time since he was wounded." The school superintendent "called on his friends at the Court House and was warmly welcomed." Hertel thanked George Fiedler, whose intervention prevented the "assailant" from getting off a second shot.

While the bullet remained in Hertel's body because the attending physicians "were unable to find it," he nonetheless recovered. The *Encyclopedia of Illinois and History of St. Clair County*, published in 1907, contains a summary of Wyatt's lynching. After noting that "the jail was pretty badly injured" by the lynch mob that broke "nearly all the windows" and left "the doors badly battered," the authors estimate the monetary cost of the destruction at between $300 and $400. "Fortunately," the narrative concludes, "Mr. Hertel recovered from his wound."

The *New York Times* reporter called the day of Wyatt's lynching "the most exciting day Belleville has known for years." The headline of this article reads: "Illinois Lynching Horror" and carries the subhead "Negro Teacher Tortured by Mob." The reporter's use of "exciting" to describe the day that a mob lynched a Black man is a curious choice of words.

The account describes Wyatt's torture and murder in explicit detail: "The mob hanged Wyatt to a telephone pole in the public square. Even while his body was jerking in the throes of death from strangulation, members of the mob began building a fire at the foot of the pole. The flames flared up and licked at the feet of the victim, but this did not satisfy the mob, and another and larger fire was started."

But even a larger fire didn't satiate this mob's bloodlust. A more fiendish death for Wyatt was quickly devised:

> *When it had begun burning briskly, the negro, still half alive, was cut down, and, after being covered with coal oil, was cast into the fire. Moans of pain were heard from the half-dead victim of the mob, and these served further to infuriate his torturers. They fell upon him with clubs and knives and cut and beat the burning body almost to pieces, and not until every sign of life had departed did they desist and permit the flames to devour the body.*

The *New York Times* report indicates that even Wyatt's death didn't placate the lynch mob. The teacher's murderers weren't satisfied with anything less than the complete destruction of his corpse: "As the fire lighted up the scene the members of the mob stood around the funeral pyre hurling more fagots of wood into the flames and denouncing the negro for the shooting. Not until the body had been reduced to ashes did the mob depart."

The *New York Times* reporter described the day as "exciting," but the reporter who covered Wyatt's lynching for the *St. Louis Post-Dispatch* saw the mob members exhibit an eerie detachment. Wyatt's murderers were neither "enthused" nor "enraged." Indeed they demonstrated a "cool, indifferent manner" that one hardly expected to see at a lynching. "It's just a way we have here in Belleville," one onlooker told the reporter.

News of Wyatt's lynching spread quickly. The murder scene became an immediate tourist attraction for those with an appetite for horror. According to the *New York Times*, "Fully 10,000 strangers visited the public square and viewed the site of the lynching. Crowds came from all sections of Southern Illinois, Missouri, Arkansas, and Kentucky. Only the charred telephone pole and bits of unconsumed flesh of the unfortunate wretch Wyatt remained for their view."

Cha-Jua quoted this succinct conclusion to the *East St. Louis Journal's* account of Wyatt's lynching. "Before the body was entirely consumed the police managed to work up sufficient energy to bring up a few pails of water," the reporter observed. "The flames were extinguished and what was left of the body was gathered up and taken to Holdener & Co. undertaking company." This reporter also made an editorial comment that "the negro richly deserved punishment." Wyatt's funeral was held a few days later and attended only by members of his immediate family. He left behind a wife and four children.

The *New York Times* reporter noted that the murder site held a special attraction for Belleville residents. "Almost every citizen of Belleville visited the scene of the lynching to-day, and not one word was heard against the action of the mob in compelling Wyatt to expiate for his terrible crime."

Once again, the reporter's choice of words is rather curious. The mob possessed neither the legal nor moral authority to compel Wyatt "to expiate" for shooting Hertel. The men who strangled, burned and hacked Wyatt to death were in no way authorized to function as his judge, jury and executioners. The fact that "not one word was heard against the action of the mob" in no way legitimized the murder. The American judicial system is not based on popular consensus.

The June 6, 1903 edition of the *Belleville News-Democrat* carried an account of the shooting that deliberately inflamed public opinion against Wyatt. The subheadline reads "Dastardly Deed Committed by a Negro," which is followed by a six-line summation of the article that refers to Wyatt as "the Black Brute."

Black citizens of Belleville were harassed and threatened on the street by white residents during the days following Wyatt's lynching. The June 9,

1903 edition of the *Alton Evening Telegraph* carried an article headlined: "Race War Imminent." The article's multiple subheadlines include "Retaliation Is Threatened" and "The Five Hundred Residents of the City Refuse the Warning to Leave." The text of the article neglects to mention precisely by whom this warning was issued. The journalist noted in his report, however, that Belleville's Black citizenry "persist in staying in spite of the lynching of Wyatt, although they know that their lives are unsafe while the present excitement lasts."

The subheadline "Retaliation Is Threatened" was drawn from a statement in the article. The reporter stated that Wyatt's "friends, both here and in all parts of St. Clair county, are threatening retribution to the instigators and leaders of the mob if their identity can be established." No quotations from Wyatt's allegedly menacing friends are provided to corroborate such a bold statement, however. After declaring, "It is impossible to describe the level of race prejudice which exists here as a result of the shooting of Superintendent Hertel," the reporter assured readers that "only a spark is needed to cause an explosion."

The "imminent" race war of which the *Alton Evening Telegraph* reporter warned never materialized. Belleville's ministers denounced the lynching from their respective pulpits. Illinois governor Richard Yates Jr., who was in Berlin at the time of the lynching, expressed his outrage in a cable. According to the June 25, 1903 edition of the *Alton Evening Telegraph*, Yates stated: "Lynching is unpardonable; it is anarchy; the leaders of the Belleville mob should be sent to the penitentiary; I will see that they stay there."

Yates was never afforded the opportunity to see that the lynching's ringleaders stayed in the penitentiary. Although a grand jury met secretly during the months of September and October, none of the nearly eighty witnesses it summoned named a single person who had participated in Wyatt's lynching. Nonetheless, the grand jury issued a total of fourteen indictments—but for rioting and assault, not murder. On the advice of counsel, eleven of the indicted men entered a guilty plea to a single charge of rioting. Each of the men was fined fifty dollars and court costs. Such a light sentence persuaded two of the other defendants to plead guilty during the court's spring session. Downey wrote that the last defendant, who maintained his innocence and refused to hire a lawyer, evidently had charges against him dropped. No one went to trial for the murder of David Wyatt.

This miscarriage of justice has not been forgotten. The *St. Louis American* published an article in 2014 titled "Belleville aka Lynchville

200th Anniversary Not All Festive." James Ingram, its author, sardonically observed: "How civil of Mayor Kern (then) and how convenient for Belleville, Ill. (now) to ignore yet another episode in its 200-year history of sordid and repeated racial strife. Happy 200th anniversary, Belleville. Here's hoping that the next 200 years will be racism and lynch-free."

THE BRIEF BUT WILD HISTORY OF BENBOW CITY

Jesse W. Ford, a resident of Anacortes, Washington, whose father was a law enforcement officer in Benbow City, wrote a memoir for the *Wood River (IL) Journal* in 1974 that included his recollections of a short-lived community of saloons and brothels known as Benbow City. One account in particular neatly summed up this long-gone town. A former Wood River alderman told Ford that when he was a "young buck," he finally mustered up the courage to venture from nearby Wood River to Benbow City. The young buck was promptly assaulted by a gang of toughs who would have beaten him to death had Ford's father not rescued him and personally escorted the future alderman back to Wood River.

Ford concluded that story with the comment, "At one time, Benbow City was reputed to be the toughest saloon town in the U.S." No one even vaguely familiar with its history would dispute that opinion. The founder of Benbow City, Amos Edward Benbow, named the town after himself. His story is almost as interesting as the rowdy community that bore his name.

The Benbows were a family of some distinction across the pond. John Benbow, a distant ancestor, had served as an admiral in the British navy. Amos Benbow's grandfather owned an estate in Riffle in the English county of Worchester, where he conducted the Stafford Bridge Inn. A devout member of the Church of England, he decided that three of his sons would enter the ministry. One son, Richard, had other ideas, however. When his father sent him off to prep school, Richard took a detour that led him to a ship bound for the United States.

He eventually made his way to southwestern Illinois, where he purchased a tract of land at the mouth of the Wood River. This was almost a century before the Wood River was rechanneled. It now comprises the border between Alton and East Alton. The mouth of the Wood River's old channel was—and, for that matter, still is—within the boundaries of the city of Wood River. Richard Benbow's son, Amos, was born on this tract of land on February 20, 1850.

Amos Benbow possessed a keen intellect and proved to be a good student in the region's public schools. He attended Shurtleff College in Upper Alton for three years but evidently left before receiving a degree. He taught school for six years and

Amos Benbow, the politician who founded and ruled Benbow City. *Author's collection.*

then left education to engage in real estate and politics. A staunch Democrat, Benbow served two terms as mayor of Upper Alton, which in his day was a separate community from the city of Alton. He also served as a constable, justice of the peace, assessor, collector and deputy sheriff.

Benbow was elected to the Forty-Fourth Illinois General Assembly. During President Grover Cleveland's first administration, he was appointed deputy U.S. marshal for the Illinois District, which included sixty-nine counties.

Amos Benbow cut an imposing figure: over six feet tall and weighing in excess of two hundred pounds. A posthumous account of his life noted that Benbow "knew 'the political game'" thoroughly and had the "faculty of gathering around him men who would follow his leadership." A modern, skeptical reader might define such a coterie of men as cronies or even a gang. This account also mentioned that "those who engaged him in political warfare knew, when the fight was over, that they had competed with an adversary who fought so long as there was the slightest chance to win, and fought with every ounce of his energy." In other words, Amos Benbow was one of the last men anyone wanted for an enemy.

Benbow possessed a passion for politics but recognized that real estate could be much more financially lucrative. In 1907, Standard Oil began the construction of a refinery near the Wood River, which opened the following year. The work crews constructing that refinery surely would build up a powerful thirst, Benbow mused. And once the refinery became operational, its employees would appreciate a place to enjoy a cold brew and let off a little steam. He still owned that tract of land near the mouth of the Wood River where he had been born. Any number of American communities contained districts that featured saloons and brothels, but why not a town composed almost exclusively of those two institutions? Such a place surely would draw men from counties throughout southwestern Illinois and make a fortune for the farsighted man who owned the town.

Unlike Alton, which had been founded by Rufus Easton in 1818 and incorporated as a city in 1837, only a few scattered farms occupied the vicinity near the Wood River. Pioneer families in the area included the Vaughns, for whom Vaughn Hill is named, and the Gillhams, who allowed the Wood River area's first school to be built on one of their pastures. Gillham's Pasture School stood at what is now the corner of Thirteenth Street and Edwardsville Road.

Compared to the hustle and bustle of nearby Alton, life must have been tranquil indeed for these farm families. That tranquility ended when Amos Benbow had Benbow City built in 1907. The town's incorporation a year later garnered mention in the *New York Times*, a distinction ordinarily denied to small towns. Benbow City, however, was no ordinary small town.

The new community, according to that distinguished newspaper, was the "'wettest' town in Illinois and because it is the wettest it is also the richest." Benbow City had begun its corporate existence with just eighteen registered voters, a population of three hundred—and no fewer than twenty-three saloons. That translated into one saloon for every thirteen inhabitants. In addition to those twenty-three saloons, the *New York Times* noted, Benbow City contained seven brewery agencies. According to the account, each saloon and brewery agency paid $500 for an annual license, an astronomical fee at that time.

"Payments for the coming year have already been made, and the little village starts out in life with a $15,000 nest egg," the article stated. "The liquor interests have paid $50 for each man, woman and child in the village, the per capita wealth of which by reason of this revenue from the liquor interests is greater than that of any town or city in the United States," it concluded.

Repeated references to "the liquor interests" demonstrate just how controversial such a blatantly liquor-based community was in early twentieth-century America. The prohibition movement was on the march, determined to make the United States a dry nation. Modern readers can scarcely imagine how the "wettest town in Illinois" must have vexed the anti-saloon activists.

An *Alton Evening Telegraph* article about the licensing of saloons in Benbow City, which ran a day earlier than the *New York Times* piece, stated that the town had only nineteen such establishments. It also mentioned an eyebrow-raising fact somehow omitted in the *New York Times* blurb. No fewer than twelve of these nineteen saloons were owned by Anheuser-Busch. That Amos Benbow could get the St. Louis brewery giant involved in such an enterprise gives some idea of the political clout he wielded. Clearly, his influence was by no means limited to southwestern Illinois.

By September 1908, according to the *Alton Evening Telegraph*, Benbow City could boast a total of twenty-two saloons, including two owned by the long-defunct Central Brewery. This brewery had also established a cold-storage plant in the town to hold its beer until needed at the saloons. If a man was thirsty in Benbow City, it was only because he was a teetotaler and couldn't find a glass of clean water.

But Benbow City soon had a couple of neighbors. Elizabeth Haller Janssen, widow of John Janssen, sold the family farm, which lay west of the area's railroad tracks, to developer P.E. "Doc" Ashlock in 1907. Just a year later, that farmland was incorporated as the village of Wood River, while East Wood River was incorporated in 1909.

The men who built the refinery had lived—and drank—in Benbow City and Wood River during its construction. With the completion of the refinery, many of these workers left the area, and the population of both towns plummeted. The hard times for saloons compelled Amos Benbow to try to diversify Benbow City's economy.

Along with other investors, he formed the System Plows Company, a corporation with $20,000 in capital. The company's principal product was to be a revolutionary kind of plow that could plow, harrow and plant seed all at the same time. The plow's unnamed inventor had given investors a test exhibition in the spring of 1909, and the corn he had planted was allegedly twenty inches high by early July. Benbow believed in the plow enough to try to lure a steel plant to Benbow City to manufacture it.

Never one to put all his eggs in one basket, however, Amos Benbow had another plan. Benbow City's Commercial Club, which Amos Benbow controlled, passed a resolution in 1909 favoring the annexation of Benbow City by Wood River. Even with Benbow City gone, he reasoned, his ownership of such a large tract of land and political influence would make him a powerful figure in Wood River.

The System Plows Company went belly up, and the annexation deal turned sour. Amos Benbow decided that his town would stay put, duke it out with Wood River and see which community survived. The battle lines were drawn in 1910, when Wood River and East Wood River merged into one town called Wood River, which left Benbow City surrounded on three sides. Only railroad tracks and a few hundred yards of ground separated the two towns, so rivalry was inevitable. It was the form that this rivalry took that left so many area residents shaking their heads in dismay.

In his memoir for the *Wood River Journal*, Ford recalled his father, Jerome Ford, getting into a gunfight with Wood River policeman Jim Chadwick. Ford didn't mention what the fight was about but said that "when Chadwick's shoulder poked out from behind a telephone pole, pop shot him."

Demonstrating that he was a Good Samaritan as well as a good marksman, Ford took Chadwick to an Alton hospital but was nonetheless "charged by U.S. Marshals, called in to clean up Benbow City, with unnecessary use of a firearm." Benbow posted bail for Ford, and the lawman was released from the Madison County Jail. Benbow City's founder then used his political clout to get all charges against Ford dropped.

Jesse Ford didn't provide a date for this incident. Another altercation between officials of Benbow City and Wood River, however, is on record as having occurred in 1908. The *Alton Evening Telegraph* carried an account of the matter under the headline "Bad Fight at Benbow City and Wood River." The headline was no exaggeration.

The Benbow City marshal, identified only as "Baird," attempted to arrest P.E. Ashlock, who was the village president of Wood River, at Benbow City's White Elephant Saloon at 3:00 a.m. for allegedly carrying a concealed weapon. The *Alton Evening Telegraph* article noted that it was not unusual for officials of either town to carry firearms, since their police forces were quite small.

Baird had removed Ashlock's watch while searching him and was just about to relieve Ashlock of his money when the suspect broke free and fled toward Wood River. Baird pursued the fugitive and fired his revolver. One of the bullets supposedly severed a finger on Ashlock's right hand.

Ashlock indeed reached Wood River, but Baird didn't halt at the Benbow City limits. The relentless marshal finally apprehended the fugitive and began to pistol-whip him. Young Ashlock's father, J.T. Ashlock, served as the police magistrate of Wood River. The elder Ashlock came out of his house, still in his nightshirt, to save his son.

Apparently delighted to now have two victims, the Benbow City marshal compelled J.T. Ashlock to remain outside in his nightshirt while his son lay unconscious on the ground. When Baird finally allowed the elder Ashlock to return to the house to clothe himself, he followed him inside, keeping his revolver pointed at the distraught father. He then pistol-whipped Ashlock.

J.T. Ashlock journeyed to Alton to swear out a warrant for Baird's arrest on a charge of assault with intent to kill. He told a *Telegraph* reporter that his son, who remained bedridden from his injuries, intended to swear out a warrant for Baird's arrest on charges of attempted robbery and assault with intent to kill.

When not fighting with Wood River residents, Benbow City inhabitants often fought with one another. Jesse Ford recalled that "local toughs and drunks" would come to his family's home to challenge his father. One such troublemaker knocked on the door when Jerome Ford was in bed, barefoot and garbed only in long underwear. When Ford answered the door, the troublemaker stomped on the lawman's bare foot. Jesse Ford wrote that his father grabbed his "forty-eight" caliber revolver—he almost certainly meant a .45-caliber revolver, possibly an old single-action model—and struck the young tough in the face with it.

The dazed malefactor was hauled off to the Benbow City Jail, which was "two buildings south of the intersection of Ferguson and Old St. Louis Road." The hauling itself was performed by one Ford called "a giant of a rather simple man known as See See," who worshiped Ford's father because he kept him fed and even allowed him to sleep in the city jail, which was built of three-by-four timbers that had been laid flat side down and spiked together. According to an old *Telegraph* article, the jail could hold four men—and that's counting a snoring See See. Jesse Ford noted that his father was a small man, and See See would floor any malefactor the Benbow City lawman couldn't handle. See See then dragged the unconscious troublemaker "to jail by his heels as his head bounced off the ground."

Benbow City marshal was an ideal job for a lawman who liked to drink. Jesse Ford sat on his father's shoulders as the elder Ford walked his beat, a beat that invariably took him into a saloon. Marshal Ford then deposited his son "on Carsten's or Bady's bar to eat pretzels while he [Jerome Ford] drank a bucket of beer."

Benbow City was a man's town and drew men from nearby communities such as Alton and cities as far away as East St. Louis. Ford recalled men arriving and leaving on the Inter-Urban Electric Railway, which helped to make Benbow City accessible for those without automobiles or horses. Of course, the men who visited Benbow City came for more than merely a drink at the saloons.

The Benbow City Jail is on permanent display outside the Wood River Museum and Visitors Center.

Jesse Ford wrote that the first building in Benbow City was Heine Carsten's Saloon, which featured "cut-glass pretzel bowls, sawdust on the floor and a house of ill-fame upstairs—or next door, I'm not sure now." He reminisced about a madam named Mame. "She was happily and successfully married while conducting her business," Ford stated. "She was always nice to all the kids."

Part of Jerome Ford's responsibilities as a Benbow City lawman was to make certain that the town's prostitutes maintained a certain decorum. If he and his son passed a brothel where the "hostesses," as they're called in this memoir, were publicly displaying a bit too much body, "Pop would call to them to put on some clothes." Evidently, the ladies got one warning and one warning only. "If they talked back, Pop would throw a brick or rock and sometimes it would go clear through the screen door." Jesse Ford failed to mention how many hostesses were seriously injured during these encounters with his hot-tempered father. He bluntly conceded, however, "To say I matured quickly and early is understating the case."

Jerome Ford might well have been the toughest hombre in a tough town. According to a 1912 *New York Times* article, however, there was at least one instance when Benbow City's bad guys came out on top. In the wee hours of a September morning, burglars broke into four homes—and one of those homes was the residence of Jerome Ford.

These thieves cut away a screen at Michael Bushen's house and made off with a watch and a pair of trousers. Frances Beers—a most apt surname for a resident of Benbow City—heard the burglars cutting a screen at her home and frightened them away by calling for her son.

Jerome Ford was on duty until 3:00 a.m. and then went home for some well-deserved sleep. When he awoke the next day, he discovered that his best suit of clothes was missing.

Did the thieves break in while Ford was copping Zs, or did the burglars make off with the suit while he was still patrolling Benbow City's streets? Ford told the press that it must have been the latter scenario, since the thieves literally would have had to crawl over the bed where he slept to get the clothes. Those familiar with Ford's reputation tended to agree with the marshal. It is difficult to imagine any burglars, however brave and/or inebriated, risking a confrontation with a suddenly awakened Jerome Ford and his trusty .45.

The journalist who wrote the three-paragraph article for the *New York Times* made a glaring factual error that revealed his naivete about this community. He identified Benbow City as the "Standard Oil town." The oil refinery indeed was the little town's neighbor but never its master. Benbow City was Amos Benbow's town, and woe to anyone who doubted it.

Saloons and bordellos aside, however, Benbow City possessed some of the trappings of a bona fide town. In 1907, Benbow founded a school, which was located on Old St. Louis Road near the end of what is now Lorena Avenue. Named Benbow School—false modesty was never one of Amos Benbow's flaws—it had an initial enrollment of thirty students. Just a year later, Benbow School had seventy-five students, indicating either that the town's population was growing or that parents belatedly realized their children were much safer in school than running loose in Benbow City. Such a large enrollment forced Benbow School to open two additional classrooms in vacant buildings across the street. The school's first teacher was Emily Ireland Smith, who taught from 1907 to 1909. Benbow School closed in 1910, and the community's children attended the Wood River School, which opened that year.

Benbow used his influence in Washington, D.C., to have a post office assigned to the community in 1908. He earlier had hired a census taker to obtain the name of every resident of Benbow City and proudly claimed his town now had a population of 420. The Benbow City post office, Benbow announced, would provide mail service for about 1,000 people, which meant that it possessed the capacity to deliver mail to area residents beyond Benbow City's borders—such as people living in Wood River. If Benbow City could provide such a vital service, Benbow thought, perhaps his town someday could annex its archrival.

Benbow City had an additional rival at least ten times more formidable than Wood River—the Standard Oil Refinery itself. The oil behemoth coveted Benbow's community and tried to wrest it from his control in 1909 by running a Standard Oil–backed mayoral candidate against the incumbent—who just happened to be Amos Benbow. The candidates' campaigns included street brawls between thugs recruited by both sides, several gunfights and threats leveled at voters thought to be leaning toward the opposition.

Benbow campaigned for mayor while encumbered by a liability that would have destroyed the candidacy of a lesser man. He didn't live in Benbow City. In 1885, Benbow had purchased the historic Hurlbut-Messenger house at 1406 Washington Avenue in Upper Alton. Benjamin Franklin Messenger, a Union veteran of the Civil War, died that year, leaving behind his wife, Helen Boardman Messenger, and their four children. Mrs. Messenger couldn't afford to maintain the home and sold it to Benbow, who allowed her to remain as his housekeeper.

Both sides claimed victory on Election Day and hurled mutual accusations of massive voter fraud. Benbow and the Standard Oil–backed candidate, a political nonentity named Olroyd, went to court to settle the matter.

A June 2, 1909 article in the *Alton Evening Telegraph* was astonishingly frank in its analysis of Benbow City's electoral chaos. After noting that a Judge Burroughs would decide the case, the unnamed reporter stated, "It would seem an impossibility to decide the case in any way, except to call a new election, as so many irregularities crept into the movements of both sides prior to and following the election that was held, there seems to be little regularity to the whole thing."

Benbow believed that he could win a new election, if the judge so ordered one to be held, the reporter noted. He then revealed Amos Benbow's election strategy:

> *Benbow has a little game he can play that will be all his own. He can import a hundred men if he wants to into the village and keep them there 30 days and vote them at the election if he wants to do it. He owns the houses*

and he has the places to keep them. The men would doubtless be glad to stay there for their board and have a good time until they could vote.

One can almost visualize Benbow promising the area's young men an abundance of free liquor and female companionship for thirty days in exchange for their votes. His business acumen was matched by his knowledge of human nature.

This *Telegraph* reporter now turned his attention to the opposition's strategy. He made it clear that Standard Oil, the business Goliath founded by none other than John D. Rockefeller, would in all likelihood suffer a defeat at the hands of Amos E. Benbow. "The other side would be somewhat handicapped, unless the Standard Oil moved a lot of its men over into Benbow City and voted them there. Benbow controls the houses and likewise a big part of the boarding houses."

It is uncertain whether Benbow won a rigged election, Judge Burroughs decided the case in his favor or mighty Standard Oil simply conceded defeat. It is certain, however, that Amos Benbow ruled Benbow City as its mayor until the town was finally annexed by Wood River in 1917.

Why did this indomitable man, who had humbled the refinery's bosses in 1909 and undoubtedly laughed when the *New York Times* naively referred to Benbow City as the "Standard Oil town" in that 1912 article, allow the town he had created and governed with an iron hand to be annexed by this rival community? Benbow City incurred extensive damage in 1915 when the Wood River flooded, and some of the water-ravaged buildings weren't even rebuilt. But it wasn't Mother Nature that sounded the death knell for Benbow City. It was our nation's anti-saloon activists.

Amos Benbow was an astute and well-connected politician who saw the handwriting on the wall. Prohibition was coming. Benbow undoubtedly knew that Prohibition would fail to banish booze from America. It would merely drive it underground into speakeasies and dives, while bootlegging would become a major, if illicit, industry in the United States. But the era of wide-open saloons, which Benbow City embodied, was coming to an end. He had no option, except to cut his losses by merging with Wood River before Prohibition made Benbow City a ghost town.

Failing health confined him to his room at the Hurlbut-Messenger House during the last two years of his life, although his interest in politics remained unabated. Newspapers kept the old politician apprised of world events, and he could discuss current topics with visitors. The opportunist who had created Benbow City solely to make money somehow found much to admire in Woodrow Wilson, perhaps the most idealistic of all American presidents, and publicly voiced the opinion that Wilson's vision of global democracy and peace would someday triumph.

One of the most colorful politicians in Illinois history died on November 14, 1922, at age seventy-two. As Benbow approached death, a niece living in West Carrollton, Ohio, was summoned to his bedside. Benbow had been a sixty-year member of the Odd Fellows, and the lodge conducted a funeral service for its celebrated brother at the Hurlbut-Messenger home. After an additional funeral service at the Upper Alton Presbyterian Church, where Elijah Lovejoy had served as pastor almost a century earlier, Benbow was interred in the Odd Fellows lot at Oakwood Cemetery in Upper Alton.

Benbow never married and—to the best of anyone's knowledge—had no children. Upon his death, the Messenger house reverted to the ownership of Helen Boardman Messenger, who had served as his housekeeper for thirty-seven years. Mrs. Messenger obviously thought a great deal of Benbow. A 1926 family history that she commissioned to be written included an entire section devoted to Benbow but contained no mention whatsoever of her long-dead husband. One of Mrs. Messenger's granddaughters was Dorothy Horton Dromgoole, a great-aunt by marriage to the author, who shared memories of her upbringing in the Hurlbut-Messenger House.

A Washington Avenue side street just opposite the Hurlbut-Messenger House was named Benbow Avenue in honor of this unique man. It still bears that name today. The Hurlbut-Messenger House was demolished in the 1950s, and that site is now occupied by the Calvary Southern Baptist Church. No trace of Benbow City remains in present-day Wood River, although the Wood River Museum and Visitors Center features an exhibit about this fabled community. The museum also proudly displays the original jail of Benbow City in the parking lot outside the building. Visitors are typically astonished by its diminutiveness. The author has seen closets that were larger than the Benbow City Jail.

In his memoir, Jesse Ford wrote that one of his relatives formerly had the handwritten minutes of the Benbow City Council. Ford remarked, "The minutes were vivid and complete, swear words of Trustees, discussion of joints, and general city problems." In other words, these minutes were about as bawdy as Benbow City itself. Ford claimed to have read some of the minutes in about 1923 and evidently didn't know their current whereabouts when writing his recollections. The minutes of the Benbow City Council have never been recovered and probably no longer exist.

Ford concluded his memoir with the admission that, in 1974, it was no longer possible to write a complete history of Benbow City. "I am disgusted with myself for not having developed a good, written history of Benbow City when many people who knew the town were alive and still in the Wood River area." He then offered an opinion that serves as an accurate, if decidedly understated, epitaph for Amos Benbow's creation. "It was undoubtedly one of the most interesting and colorful communities ever to exist."

Well put, Mr. Ford, and so very true.

CURTIS REESE

MINISTER, HUMANIST, CRIMEFIGHTER

Historians, humanists and Unitarian Universalists recognize Curtis Reese as one of the founders of religious humanism. First Unitarian Church of Alton, Illinois, which he served as minister from 1913 to 1915, remembers Reese as a courageous reformer who risked his life to battle crime in the community served by his church.

Reese was born in 1887 on a farm in the Blue Ridge Mountains of North Carolina, and his family included many Southern Baptist stalwarts. At age nine, he confessed to the congregation that he was a sinner who trusted Christ to save his soul. Although it was winter, Reese and several other converts were baptized in a nearby creek.

Believing that God had called him to the ministry, Reese was ordained as a Baptist minister by the Mars Hill Baptist Church after graduating from the Baptist College at Mars Hill, North Carolina. He graduated from the Southern Baptist Theological Seminary at Louisville, Kentucky, in 1910 and was appointed state evangelist for the five hundred churches that made up the Illinois State Baptist Association.

Reese's faith in a literal interpretation of the Bible had been shaken by his introduction to scriptural higher criticism while attending seminary. It was also in Louisville that Reese became acquainted with Unitarianism. His doubts continued to grow while earning another degree in 1911 at Ewing College, a now-defunct Baptist school in Ewing, Illinois. Realizing that he could no longer remain a Southern Baptist, Reese became pastor of First

Baptist Church of Tiffin, Ohio, which was affiliated with the more liberal Northern Baptist denomination.

"Nevertheless," Reese later wrote, "I began to thirst for more liberty....I was tired of the restrictions of orthodoxy. I wanted the liberty of a free faith, and I was determined to find it if it existed."

Reese met with the minister of the Unitarian church in Toledo, Ohio. Their ensuing discussion convinced Reese that Unitarianism comprised the kind of "free faith" he had been seeking. A later meeting with the secretary of the Western Unitarian Conference went well, and Reese became a Unitarian minister.

His rejection of the Baptists for the Unitarians did not sit well with his family. "If you study the new testament Prairefuly [*sic*] you will find no room for Unitarian Nonsence [*sic*]," Reese's father wrote in a letter dated May 1, 1913. "For as dear as I love you I wold [*sic*] almost Rather here [*sic*] of your death than to here that you left the Baptist and gone to a Church that don't beleave [*sic*] in Jesus Crist [*sic*]." In his unpublished memoirs, Reese wrote of similarly "severe reactions" from his mother, brothers and a sister.

First Unitarian Church of Alton had been without a minister for over two years when Reese preached from the pulpit on a two-week trial basis in the spring of 1913. He was well received and accepted a call to serve as pastor, beginning in September 1913. The former Baptist soon exceeded all expectations. An article in the *Alton Evening Telegraph* noted that "eighteen new members have been added to the church" since Reese assumed the pulpit. "A new spirit permeates the whole and the church," the article

Curtis Reese, who later became a giant of the humanist movement, served as pastor of First Unitarian Church of Alton from 1913 to 1915.

concluded, "and its friends are expecting great things." Local civic boosters had no idea that these "great things" would include an anti-crime campaign led by Reese.

Alton at that time had a well-deserved reputation as a wide-open city where gambling and prostitution thrived. Public officials, some of whom were rumored to receive payoffs from gangsters, showed little interest in cleaning up the community. Even area ministers remained silent. Curtis Reese broke the silence.

Reese mobilized the city's ministers and other concerned citizens to join him in establishing an Anti-Crime Syndicate, which the Unitarian minister served as chairman. He raised money to hire a detective so that evidence could be gathered in the prosecution of Alton's gangsters. Reese began receiving threatening notes from the underworld, and gunmen fired shots at him on several occasions.

Alton's mayor despised the young reformer. On March 28, 1914, Reese sent a letter to the mayor formally demanding protection of his life and property, the first time in the city's history that a citizen had been forced to take such a drastic measure. "It has come to my attention that you have on several occasions made derogatory statements concerning me," Reese wrote, "saying…that I should be horse-whipped, run out of town, etc." Such language, the minister observed, could be interpreted by his enemies as "a license…to use force and violence with impunity." Reese concluded the letter by demanding police protection so that he "could safely walk the streets of this city and not be molested, either in my person or my property."

Reese was successful in bringing some malefactors to justice. The defendants were returning from Edwardsville, the county seat, in December 1914 after the judge granted a change of venue and postponed the proceedings until January. Reese had the misfortune of encountering the indicted gangsters at a train depot in nearby Mitchell, Illinois.

One of the gangsters seized Reese's arm and struck at his face three times. The minister successfully blocked each attempted blow. Reese told the *Alton Evening Telegraph*, which carried an account of the incident, that he believed everyone in the gang of ten or more was armed and prepared to shoot him at the slightest provocation. Otherwise, Reese told the reporter, he would have fought the assailant, since he had little regard for that particular gangster's ability as a "sparrer." Reese also told the reporter that the gangster had asked him if he carried a revolver.

The minister replied that he was unarmed but would gladly fight them one at a time. The gang continued to follow Reese around the station platform, abusing him with "foul epithets" and "threats of physical violence." When the Alton train finally arrived, several mob members boarded Reese's car and continued to threaten him. The newspaper account stated that when Reese arrived in Alton, "he was cool, and there was not an indication that he had been through any trying experience."

Such newspaper coverage fueled the campaign of the Anti-Crime Syndicate. The mayor who had said that Reese should be horsewhipped did not stand for re-election in 1915, and a reform candidate won the office. It must have been a bittersweet victory for Reese, however. On election night, a mob gathered in front of the clergyman's house and ignited several fires. Reese and his wife took refuge in the home of a parishioner.

Curtis Reese left the pulpit of First Unitarian Church of Alton in 1915 to become the minister of the First Unitarian Church in Des Moines, Iowa. During his second year at Des Moines, Reese preached what he would later describe as the first humanist sermon delivered from any pulpit in America. He and John Dietrich would be credited as the co-founders of religious humanism, and Reese contributed to the composition of the 1933 Humanist Manifesto in addition to signing that landmark document. He died in 1961.

Did Reese's experiences in Alton play a role in shaping his personal philosophy? Perhaps. In his 1931 book *Humanist Religion*, he discussed the qualities of leadership that are necessary to achieve success for a civic movement. "The worst difficulty is that the leader of a movement himself often grows weary or feels the pull in other directions," he observed. "Was the thing originally worth while? What good will it do after all?" It's quite possible that Reese asked himself those very questions when he led the Anti-Crime Syndicate in Alton.

Ironically, the city that Reese sought to rid of gambling has played host to a riverboat casino since 1991, which contributes significant tax revenue to the city's treasury.

THE EAST ST. LOUIS RACE RIOT

Some scholars have stated that the East St. Louis race riot, with its thirty-nine dead Black people and nine white, was the most lethal race riot in our nation's history until the 1992 Los Angeles riot that resulted from the acquittal of the police officers who had been videotaped beating Rodney King. They're mistaken. The East St. Louis tragedy still holds the body count record hands-down. In fact, it isn't even close.

The official tally of thirty-nine murdered Black people is ridiculously low, although arriving at a reasonable estimate is no easy task. Thousands of African Americans, most of whom were never documented, had been lured to East St. Louis during the years before the riot by the promise of plenty of well-paid jobs. Thousands fled the city after the riot, never to return. This made it all but impossible to determine how many members of the African American community were missing and should be presumed dead. It is also a terrible fact that some—children and even infants—were incinerated in fires set by white mobs.

Some of these victims were killed by gunshots. Others were literally burned alive. There were also numerous reports of bullet-riddled Black corpses tossed by white mobs into the Mississippi. They were the fortunate ones. As Black families tried to flee across the Free Bridge (now known as the MacArthur Bridge) to the relative safety of St. Louis, some were overtaken by white assailants and thrown into the river. No corpses were recovered from the swift, muddy waters.

A St. Clair County grand jury set the death toll at close to one hundred. Reporters for the *St. Louis Argus*, a Black newspaper based in St. Louis, as well as reporters for the area's major dailies, maintained that over one hundred African Americans were killed. Investigators sent to East St. Louis by the NAACP and the *Chicago Defender*, the nation's most prominent Black newspaper, placed the fatalities between one and two hundred. The shocking truth is that we will never know precisely how many African American men, women and children were murdered during the East St. Louis race riot.

Rampaging white mobs and even police officers attacked newspaper photographers, smashed their cameras and deliberately exposed the film. Crazed with racial hatred, these murderers still possessed enough sanity to try to ensure there would be no record of their actions. There is a photo on page 130 of Harper Barnes's *Never Been a Time: The 1917 Race Riot That Sparked the Civil Rights Movement* with the caption "Blacks fleeing East St. Louis." Unfortunately, however, it merely depicts men and women carrying bundles and other items walking along a sidewalk. There is only a hint of the unfolding tragedy. A man holding a large bundle is looking back, as though to determine whether he and the others are being pursued.

Another photo of the riot depicts a crowd of men converging on an East St. Louis streetcar. Most of the men can be identified as civilians by the white shirts they're wearing. A few men are obviously garbed in the distinctive uniforms of the National Guard and can be seen bearing the bolt-action Springfield rifles that were standard issue in 1917.

Still, the photo is a long shot and it's impossible to discern what is occurring around the streetcar. One has to read *Never Been a Time* or Elliot Rudwick's *Race Riot at East St. Louis, July 2, 1917* to learn that the white mob was dragging African Americans from the streetcar. Some were beaten into unconsciousness and then left alone. Others were beaten into unconsciousness and then shot to death. Most National Guardsmen were simply bystanders, merely watching what was unfolding before their eyes. They made no effort to stop the rampaging mob and protect the embattled African American passengers. Some guardsmen in East St. Louis eventually threw in with the rioters and joined them in killing African Americans.

In order to understand why the riot occurred, it is necessary to delve into American race relations during the late nineteenth and early twentieth centuries and how these dynamics affected East St. Louis. In exchange for southern support to put Rutherford B. Hayes in the White House after the disputed election of 1876, the GOP—the party of Lincoln—agreed to end Reconstruction. Through legislation and outright terrorism, Black southerners were gradually disenfranchised and thrust into a state not far removed from the slavery that had supposedly been abolished by the Thirteenth Amendment, which was written by Senator Lyman Trumbull, the Illinois Republican.

Black newspapers, such as the *Chicago Defender*, urged African Americans to leave the South and move to the northern states. The factories were booming, jobs were to be had and the northern political climate, while not free of racial bigotry, was far less toxic than anything found in the lynch-happy South.

And leave they did. Between 1910 and 1920, at least half a million Black people moved north, about 400,000 of that number in the second half of the decade. While no few had been encouraged to leave Dixie by letters from relatives who had moved North, there was another group involved in expediting this great migration—and it did not have the best interests of African Americans at heart.

Steel mills and other industries wanted a large labor force that would serve to drive down wages and undermine unions. While the radical Industrial Workers of the World sought to organize all workers regardless of race, religion or ethnicity, unions belonging to the American Federation of Labor barred Black workers. A huge influx of African Americans who were ignored by organized labor ensured that industrialists would have a ready supply of strikebreakers at their disposal.

In 1916, three dozen men were fired from Swift, Morris and Armour meatpacking plants in National City, a company town just outside of East St. Louis, for trying to organize a union. When more than four thousand men went out on strike in protest, management brought in hundreds of Black strikebreakers and succeeded in destroying the organizing drive.

Management at the Aluminum Ore Company, also located just outside of East St. Louis, began laying off union workers that year and replacing them with Black laborers, who would work for meager wages. These displaced union workers, many of whom lived in East St. Louis, now looked on African Americans as their enemies. Anger that should have been directed at management instead was aimed at fellow workers of another race.

The Democratic Party also bore no small degree of responsibility for the race riot. Woodrow Wilson, elected to the presidency in 1912, fired a number of high-ranking Black federal officials who had served under the preceding GOP administrations and replaced them with white appointees. He also allowed his cabinet members to segregate their departments. Our nation's capital, which had been relatively integrated under the Republicans, became segregated under the Democrats.

Wilson had won election in 1912 largely because William Howard Taft and Teddy Roosevelt split the Republican vote at a time when the GOP was the majority party in the United States. In 1916, the Republicans however, had reunited under the candidacy of Charles Evans Hughes, so Wilson was faced with a tough reelection campaign. African Americans of that era voted overwhelmingly for the party of Lincoln. Wilson's campaign managers decided to try to win swing states such as Illinois by playing to the fears of many white voters that the Republicans would use the large number of Black citizens who had so recently migrated north to steal the election for the GOP.

The *East St. Louis Daily Journal*, which backed Wilson and the Democrats, ran a series of sensationalistic articles about "black colonizers" who were supposedly responsible for a crime wave in the city. Even the unions contributed to community fears when an AFL organizer claimed that Black rapists made it unsafe for East St. Louis white women to visit their next-door neighbors after dark. Rumors spread that a large number of Black voters would vote at dawn in Chicago and board a south-bound train, disembark in central Illinois to vote again and then ride the train to East St. Louis to vote a third time. Dr. Leroy H. Bundy, a prominent African American dentist who lived in East St. Louis, was arrested and interrogated in the Windy City as the alleged ringleader of this plot. Bundy was released for lack of evidence, but the *East St. Louis Daily Journal* gave his arrest front-page coverage, further fueling white fears that East St. Louis Black voters were part of a conspiracy to steal the presidential election for the Republicans.

Wilson narrowly won reelection but lost Illinois to Hughes. It seemed to confirm the worst suspicions of white East St. Louisans that their city's African Americans indeed must have been partners in a conspiracy to place Illinois in the GOP column on Election Day.

The town was known as the "Pittsburgh of the West," a nickname that gave the impression East St. Louis possessed a solid industrial base. Actually, nothing could have been further from the truth. Industrialists established company towns around East St. Louis to avoid paying taxes to the city's treasury. East Coast money built the St. Louis National Stockyards on unincorporated land just north of the East St. Louis city limits. Armour and Swift also moved in to process meat from livestock pens that could accommodate as many as ten thousand sheep, fifteen thousand cattle and twenty thousand hogs. When East St. Louis began annexing unincorporated land, the Meat Trust protected its interests by setting up the company town of National City, with a mayor handpicked by the Meat Trust as well as a tax assessor who was an employee of a meatpacking house. Other company towns near East St. Louis included Alorton, created by the Aluminum Ore Company, and Monsanto, later known as Sauget, set up by the chemical company of the same name.

Many East St. Louisans drew paychecks from these companies, but the City of East St. Louis couldn't collect a penny in taxes from them. There were, however, two enterprises that thrived within the city limits: saloons and brothels. How important was booze to the economy of East St. Louis? Revenue from saloon licenses in the St. Louis, Missouri, of 1916 composed about 4.5 percent of that city's annual budget. By contrast, money derived in 1916 from saloon licenses in East St. Louis amounted to $175,000, which was 43 percent of the city's $400,000 for the year.

The $175,000 figure doesn't include revenue derived from "blind tigers," which were unlicensed saloons that operated outside the law. Proprietors of these establishments paid money not to the city treasury but directly into the pockets of East St. Louis police and politicians. When local ministers and other reform-minded citizens lodged complaints about blind tigers, the police would periodically shut down some of them. A few well-placed bribes later, these saloons would invariably reopen. In East St. Louis, it was never a question of whether the police were on the take but, rather, to what degree they were on the take. A police officer's salary was just $70 to $80 a month, so bribes from blind tigers and brothels were a necessity.

Booze flowed freely in East St. Louis, although all the licensed saloons and blind tigers combined were not nearly enough to keep the town financially solvent. City hall in 1917—the year of the riot—raised the annual saloon license from $500 to $750 in an attempt to get the town's financial ledger out of the red.

Corruption was a way of life in the city. In 1916, a *St. Louis Post-Dispatch* reporter wrote a series of articles lambasting East St. Louis mayor Fred Mollman and Police Chief Ransom Payne for turning a blind eye toward their city's gambling and prostitution. Mollman, up for reelection in 1917, closed the Commercial Hotel, a center for gambling and prostitution located just two blocks from city hall, to placate the reformers. The place reopened shortly after Mollman was reelected to office on April 3, 1917.

In 1917, tensions between white and Black factions often led to fist and stone-throwing fights between street gangs. Racism in East St. Louis was evident even on the police force. The six African Americans on the seventy-man force were all plainclothesmen, since it was believed that the very sight of Black men in police uniforms would outrage white East St. Louisans.

For a three-day run, the Majestic Theater in downtown East St. Louis played D.W. Griffith's racist masterpiece *The Birth of a Nation* in February 1917. White families packed the theater to watch Caucasian actors in blackface menace virginal white women in a Black-ruled Reconstruction South. Audience members wondered whether such atrocities would occur in East St. Louis when Black migration to their city finally made white residents the minority race.

The monstrous July race riot was preceded by a minor riot in late May. Mollman presided at a city council meeting that was packed with white citizens alarmed by a crime wave supposedly instigated by Black migrants. The embattled mayor promised to do what he could to stem the tide of African American migration to the city. By all accounts, some members of the crowd were stirred to a frenzy by an address from Alexander Flannigen, a former city treasurer who, in true East St. Louis tradition, had enriched himself with public funds while in office. Flannigen left no doubt regarding how he thought white East St. Louisans should deal with this influx of Black people.

"As far as I know," he said, "there is no law against mob violence." Besides, he continued, even if such a law existed, the police could hardly arrest an entire mob. Much of the audience rose to applaud and cheer, while Mollman and some local labor leaders tried to maintain order.

Flannigen's inflammatory remarks induced fifty to one hundred men and women to leave city hall, where they were met by a crowd with news

The long-derelict Majestic Theater in East St. Louis played the film *The Birth of a Nation*, which glorifies the Reconstruction-era Ku Klux Klan for twentieth-century Americans. *Photo by East St. Louis native Bob Gill.*

that a Black stick-up artist had wounded a white man. The crowd became further enraged upon seeing police officers with handcuffed Black suspects. A gang of white men broke away from the crowd and began moving down Collinsville Avenue in search of African Americans to assault.

Black bystanders were accosted and beaten. A mob of white men seized a Black man and held him down across a trolley track while urging the trolley driver to run him over. The trolley driver did not comply. Two plainclothes detectives drew their service revolvers and stopped a mob from setting fire to a row of Black-owned homes, but most police officers did little or nothing to deter white attacks on Black citizens. Instead, they concentrated on confiscating firearms from Black residents, who were carrying handguns as a defense.

Mollman closed all saloons, theaters and schools the next day and ordered the police to arrest all groups of men larger than five. The National Guard arrived just as the riot flared up again, with white vigilantes setting fire to Black neighborhoods and throwing stones and bricks at any African American on the street. Black and white shooters exchanged gunshots just north of downtown.

No one was killed during the May 26–27 riot, but isolated incidents of violence continued into June. An elderly Black man was beaten almost to death by a white gang when he refused to give up his seat on a streetcar to a white woman. Union workers beat Black strikebreakers outside of Aluminum Ore.

African Americans began arming themselves in anticipation of another riot. Mollman had prohibited East St. Louis pawnshops from selling guns to Black people, so a lively smuggling business soon got underway. Since police frisked all African Americans who returned from St. Louis, a few African Americans who could pass for white made money bringing firearms from the Gateway City. Barnes reported that Black-owned funeral homes with hearses that traveled between the two cities sometimes stashed guns in coffins.

East St. Louis white citizens probably knew nothing about this firearms smuggling but believed rumors that Black people were planning a July Fourth uprising. Conversely, African Americans believed that white aggressors intended to massacre everyone who attended a Black Fourth of July celebration in an East St. Louis city park. The town was a tinderbox—and some random shootings on the night of July 1 provided the spark.

A gang of white men in a car drove through a Black neighborhood and fired shots into houses. A short time later, another white gang in a car followed suit. When a police car was dispatched to investigate, it was fired on by Black residents. One of the officers was killed immediately, while another died two days later. A third officer suffered a wound to his right arm.

In a deliberately provocative action, authorities allowed the bullet-riddled car to be left parked just across the street from the police station. Angry white citizens, some drinking, gathered to look at the vehicle. They began talking about taking revenge on the city's African Americans. A white mob that gathered at the city's Labor Temple was harangued by Richard Brockway, a security guard for a streetcar company. Brockway concluded his tirade with the vow, "We're going to get some niggers today." He then marched from the Labor Temple, followed by some men. A few minutes later, they chanced upon a Black man. Brockway fired five bullets into him.

By 11:00 a.m., Black East St. Louisans were being beaten and murdered from the southern section of downtown to St. Clair Avenue—an area comprising over a square mile. Robert Boylan, a *St. Louis Globe-Democrat* reporter, stated that white crowds were pursing Black people "like boys chasing rabbits." Boylan also saw white prostitutes, wearing kimonos and silk stockings, chasing a Black woman who held a little boy by the hand. She finally picked up the child and fled into a shanty. The prostitutes, their faces still wearing the heavy makeup of the previous night, then pelted the shanty with coal chunks.

Illinois National Guardsmen, summoned to quell the riot, proved to be as racist as the mobs. G.E. Popkess, a reporter for the *East St. Louis Daily Journal*, heard a guardsman asked a rioter, "Got your nigger yet?" Some National Guardsmen joined in the carnage by shooting Black citizens with their 30.06-caliber Springfield rifles.

An elderly Black man, pursued by a white mob, ran to some guardsmen for protection. They leveled their bayonets at the man to deliberately force him back into the mob, where he was beaten and kicked to death. The next day, in a Black-owned funeral parlor, the old man's arms, stiffened from rigor mortis, still shielded his face.

White rioters shot Black people as they fled from burning buildings. African Americans were hanged from light or telephone poles. One man survived hanging and was sitting on the steps of a drugstore with the rope still around his neck. A white man noticed him, walked over to where he was sitting and shot him dead.

The rioters traveled in small groups without apparent leadership. They exhibited no signs of frenzy, moving with a cool deliberateness. Many white onlookers watched the rioters while they assaulted Black citizens, either remaining silent or cheering and applauding their actions. A few white East St. Louisans sheltered their Black neighbors, undoubtedly saving their lives. Armed Black residents tried to protect their neighborhoods when they realized that they could expect no help from the East St. Louis police or National Guard.

Colonel Stephen Tripp, who commanded the guardsmen dispatched to East St. Louis, had spent most of his army career as a quartermaster and possessed no combat experience. He arrived in East St. Louis wearing a business suit, rather than a uniform. Castigated for his incompetency by the congressional committee established to investigate the riot, Tripp failed to organize the guardsmen or even to give them clear orders concerning what they were expected to do. It was only when Lieutenant Colonel E.P. Clayton, an experienced commander, took charge that the National Guard began restoring order in East St. Louis. Mollman was also criticized by the congressional committee for his weak leadership, while the East St. Louis police force was assailed for destroying newspaper photographers' cameras and threatening them with arrest if they tried to document what was occurring.

Area industrialists also bore blame for the riot, according to the congressional committee, since their deliberate use of African American strikebreakers served to pit Black labor against white labor.

W.E.B. DuBois, the Black sociologist and historian, journeyed from New York to East St. Louis to investigate the riot for the NAACP. He blamed much of the racial tension that led to the riot on area industrialists' use of Black strikebreakers but argued that the American labor movement also bore responsibility for its failure to allow Black workers into its unions.

Oscar Leonard, the superintendent of the Jewish Educational and Charitable Association of St. Louis, characterized the riot as a pogrom, the term used to describe the massacre of Jews in czarist Russia. He also stated that a Russian Jewish immigrant had told him that Russian anti-Semites could take lessons in perpetrating a pogrom from the white citizens of East St. Louis.

The East St. Louis riot electrified the entire civil rights movement. Membership in the NAACP stood at just 9,200 in 1917. One year later, membership had soared to almost 44,000. Circulation of the *Crisis*, the organization's house organ, exceeded 50,000, due in no small part to Dubois's impassioned articles about the riot.

A city where saloons, blind tigers, gambling dens and brothels abounded was virtually guaranteed to attract the very worst elements of American

Left: W.E.B DuBois journeyed to East St. Louis to investigate the riot for the NAACP.

Above: Demonstrations took place across the United States to protest the riot. This march took place in New York City. *Public domain photo from the* Crisis, *published by the NAACP.*

society. During the years before the riot, a plethora of petty criminals moved to East St. Louis because of its reputation as a wide-open town where civic and judicial corruption were the accepted norm. And they were armed and dangerous. A handgun could be purchased in the downtown pawnshops for as little as fifty cents. This does not mean that East St. Louis lacked decent, hardworking folks. Still, a city that derived 43 percent of its revenue from saloons could not be expected to produce or attract an overabundance of model citizens.

While the town's lowlife element made up a sizable portion of the mobs that murdered Black residents, they were joined by what society often terms perfectly respectable people: an ice wagon driver, a railroad switchman, a messenger boy and too many others to list. Thousands of others, while not participating in the mayhem, watched the beatings and murders and even cheered and applauded. Why? Scholars who grapple with this question postulate that when a mob psychology becomes dominant, it allows people to commit or at least applaud acts that they normally would find morally repellent. Jazz great Miles Davis, who grew up in East St. Louis long after the riot, stated that he always knew that most East St. Louis white residents were "racist to the bone." The mob psychology that ruled East St. Louis on July 2, 1917, unleashed that racism with horrifying results.

Racism hampered the prosecution of those brought to trial for crimes committed during the riots. Very few white East St. Louisans would admit under oath to having seen any fellow citizens commit acts of violence on

July 2. Six policemen, charged with murder or conspiracy to murder, were offered a sweetheart deal: the murder charges were dropped in exchange for any three of the six pleading guilty to a single charge of rioting. The six officers drew numbers from a hat to determine who would plead guilty. All six pitched in to pay the fine—just $150—set by Judge George A. Crow, a longtime political hack. The *St. Louis Argus* denounced the deal and said that Crow's ruling effectively set the fine for killing a Black person in East St. Louis at just $50.

Thirteen African American men were prosecuted for the murder of the officer who was killed when fired on in the unmarked police car that drove through a Black neighborhood. Crow barred the defense from allowing Black witnesses to testify about the carloads of white gangs that entered Black neighborhoods and fired on homes. An all-white jury found ten of the defendants guilty, and Crow sentenced them to a minimum of fourteen years at the Menard State Prison in Chester, Illinois.

Many white residents of southwestern Illinois—even those who live in the St. Louis and Metro East area—are unfamiliar with the East St. Louis race riot. That is certainly not the case with the area's African American population, however. Southern Illinois University at Edwardsville professor emeritus Eugene Redmond, the official poet laureate of East St. Louis, stated that there has never been a time when the riot was not alive in the Black oral tradition. A tragedy of such magnitude must remain alive in the conscience of every American.

This cartoon, which ran in the *New York Evening Mail*, carried this caption: "Mr. President, why not make America safe for democracy?" *Wikipedia Commons.*

The city of East St. Louis has erected interpretative signs along the path of the riot. *Photo by East St. Louis native Bob Gill.*

THE LYNCHING OF ROBERT PRAGER

A WORLD WAR I HATE CRIME

A t least one hundred African Americans were lynched during the 1917 East St. Louis race riot. The following year, a German immigrant named Robert Paul Prager was hanged by a mob, the victim of the anti-German hysteria on the homefront during World War I.

Born in Dresden, Germany, in 1888, Prager immigrated to the United States in 1905 for the better opportunities that he thought would be afforded him in this country. In 1918, the unmarried German was working the night shift in a Maryville coal mine when he sought membership in the United Mine Workers of America local, since it would have brought him a higher salary and possible career advancement.

Prager's application was swiftly rejected, possibly because he was an active socialist who had promulgated that ideology to other miners in the area. The conservative leadership of the union local evidently decided to discredit this bothersome socialist agitator by denouncing him as a German spy who had been sent to southwestern Illinois to disrupt America's war effort by sabotaging its mines.

The charge was utterly ludicrous, of course. One of the men with whom Prager boarded later affirmed that, while he was indeed a radical socialist and not yet an American citizen, Prager had stated he was "all for the United States" when our nation declared war on Germany in 1917. It later came to light that Prager actually had a St. Louis baker arrested when he objected to Prager's display of an American flag. The baker was jailed for thirty-two days.

Unfortunately, Prager had unwittingly given what appeared to be corroboration to the accusation of disloyalty. He had recently asked his co-workers about the effects of certain explosives as he sought to acquaint himself with the responsibilities of a mine manager. His innocent interest in such matters easily lent itself to distortion by the anti-German prejudice of that era.

Outraged by such vile accusations, Prager posted a number of handbills in the Maryville-Collinsville area that vehemently denied he was a spy and affirmed his loyalty to the United States. But sufficient suspicion had been planted in the minds of many of Prager's fellow miners, and they decided he merited some rough justice.

On the afternoon of April 4, Prager was seized by several miners who manhandled the diminutive German and forced him to kiss the flag. After a few anxious moments, Prager managed to break free from his assailants and fled to his residence. This incident was just a precursor of much worse things to come.

A company of miners gathered that evening in a tavern on Collinsville's outskirts to discuss what should be done about the disloyal miner Prager, who advocated socialism while in the Kaiser's pay. Like Prager, most of the miners were foreign-born. Unlike Prager, however, these miners spoke little English and probably found it difficult to understand precisely what Prager was alleged to have said and done. Based on faulty knowledge, they decided that Prager was disloyal to the United States and deserved to be punished.

Shortly after 9:00 p.m., these miners—now quite intoxicated—burst into Prager's residence at 208½ Vandalia in Collinsville and dragged him into the street. They had no particular intention of murdering Prager at this time, however. He was merely forced to kiss the flag again and then walk barefoot through Collinsville while draped in Old Glory.

Much to the disgust of the crowd, which may have swelled to as many as three hundred after a time, a motorcycle police officer rescued the disheveled German and took him to city jail for his own safety. Collinsville mayor John H. Siegel ordered all the city's taverns closed in the hope that tempers would subside. The police officer who was dispatched to close the saloons only made matters worse, however, by announcing in each tavern that a German spy was incarcerated in the city jail.

A mob soon gathered outside of the city jail. Now desperate, the embattled Siegel and his law enforcement officers decided to try to placate the hooligans by hiding Prager in the jail basement, informing the mob that he had been transferred to East St. Louis and then allowing Joseph Riegel, an army veteran and cobbler/miner who was one of the mob's ringleaders, to search the jail as proof.

The ruse almost worked. Seeing Prager's empty cell placated the mob that burst into the building with Riegel, and the men began to leave the building. Suddenly, some hooligans whose minds were not completely clouded from liquor realized that Prager couldn't have possibly been transferred to another city while the jail was surrounded by several hundred people. The search for the German was abruptly resumed, and Prager was discovered hiding under some tiles in the basement.

The performance of Collinsville's finest in the face of this challenge to law and order almost defies belief. One police officer later testified at the inquest that he made no attempt to save Prager as the mob led him from the jail because the phone rang and he had to answer it. Another officer stated that he and some fellow officers had followed the gang from the jail only to ensure that the lynching was not performed in the city limits. If that indeed was the case, then the Collinsville Police Department was successful: Prager was brutally marched down St. Louis Road and out of town to a tree atop Bluff Road for his hanging.

There is some evidence to suggest that the mob originally intended merely to tar and feather Prager. When Prager was captured at the Collinsville jail, an auto mechanic named Harry Lindemann arrived driving an automobile. Several mob members jumped aboard the car and ordered Lindemann to drive to a nearby farm, where they believed some tar and feathers could be obtained. It's uncertain whether the farm could be located or simply lacked tar and feathers. The car and its passengers returned to Collinsville and met the mob, which still had Prager as its prisoner.

The headlights of three automobiles illuminated the scene as Prager, held captive under the tree from which he would shortly hang, was questioned for about twenty minutes. He continued to deny that he was a spy for Imperial Germany or had any intention of blowing up area mines. Then, according to Riegel, "someone tied the rope around his neck and a lot of boys from twelve to sixteen years old pulled him up."

Another account, however, has Riegel initially attempting to pull the rope solo. He then purportedly chided the others present as "slackers" and reminded them that they were all in this together. Riegel shortly had assistance from other mob members in pulling the rope.

But the murderers had overlooked a rather important detail: They had neglected to tie the poor wretch's hands. "His hands were not tied, and he grabbed at the rope," Riegel later conceded. "They let him down."

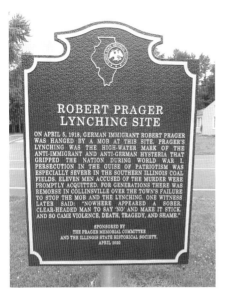

ROBERT PRAGER
LYNCHING SITE

ON APRIL 5, 1918, GERMAN IMMIGRANT ROBERT PRAGER
WAS HANGED BY A MOB AT THIS SITE. PRAGER'S
LYNCHING WAS THE HIGH-WATER MARK OF THE
ANTI-IMMIGRANT AND ANTI-GERMAN HYSTERIA THAT
GRIPPED THE NATION DURING WORLD WAR I.
PERSECUTION IN THE GUISE OF PATRIOTISM WAS
ESPECIALLY SEVERE IN THE SOUTHERN ILLINOIS COAL
FIELDS. ELEVEN MEN ACCUSED OF THE MURDER WERE
PROMPTLY ACQUITTED. FOR GENERATIONS THERE WAS
REMORSE IN COLLINSVILLE OVER THE TOWN'S FAILURE
TO STOP THE MOB AND THE LYNCHING. ONE WITNESS
LATER SAID: "NOWHERE APPEARED A SOBER,
CLEAR-HEADED MAN TO SAY 'NO' AND MAKE IT STICK.
AND SO CAME VIOLENCE, DEATH, TRAGEDY, AND SHAME."

SPONSORED BY
THE PRAGER MEMORIAL COMMITTEE
AND THE ILLINOIS STATE HISTORICAL SOCIETY.
APRIL 2020

This commemorative plaque marking the site of Prager's lynching was dedicated in 2020.

Thus granted this brief reprieve, Prager asked to kiss an American flag, uttered a quick prayer in German and wrote a short note of farewell to his parents in Germany. Written in his native tongue, the translated note reads: "Dear Parents: I must die on April 4, 1918. Please pray for me, my dear parents. This is my last letter and testament. Your dear son and brother, Robert Paul Prager."

Ironically, Prager's letter was brought to the offices of the *Collinsville Herald* shortly after his lynching by none other than Joseph Riegel.

Upon completing this letter, Prager was asked again to reveal his partners in the spy ring to which he allegedly belonged. When he remained silent, someone in the crowd shouted, "Well, if he won't tell, string him up!"

The courageous German was said to have replied, "All right, boys, go ahead and kill me, but wrap me in the flag when you bury me."

The mob had learned its lesson. This time, Prager's hands were tied with an old handkerchief. The rope was pulled, and Prager was lifted off the ground.

Testifying at the inquest, Riegel recalled that the crowd had grown rather uneasy after watching Prager dangling in the air for a time, so it was decided to conclude the incident as quickly as possible. The rope, which had been secured to a telephone pole, was pulled, raising Prager to the highest branches of the tree. Then the rope was abruptly dropped three times— "One for the red! One for the white! One for the blue!"—as someone in the crowd shouted with each plunge the German took.

Robert Paul Prager died of strangulation at approximately 12:30 a.m. His lifeless body was left to dangle a half hour before finally being lowered.

Prager's courage and fortitude in the face of certain death made an impression on one of his killers. "Brother, that was the bravest guy I ever saw in my life," Riegel admitted. "He never shed a tear, except when he kissed the flag, and did not once beg for mercy or ask us to turn him loose."

But not everyone shared Riegel's grudging admiration for the martyred German. The late Irving Dillard, a Collinsville resident and author who served as editor of the editorial page of the *St. Louis Post-Dispatch*, was thirteen at the time of this tragedy and remembered seeing Prager's body in the Herr Undertaking Parlor the morning after his murder. Dillard recalled hearing someone in the line of curiosity-seekers waiting to see the German's corpse joke that everyone should look at the rope marks on Prager's neck that showed "in red, white and blue."

Illinois public office holders did not take so flippant a view of the lynching. U.S. senator Lawrence Y. Sherman denounced Collinsville as well as East St. Louis as the "Sodom and Gomorrah of Illinois" and castigated Prager's murderers as a "drunken mob masquerading in the garb of patriots." Illinois governor Frank Lowden was outraged by Prager's murder and had the adjunct attorney-general alerted to declare martial law if necessary. The lynching was even brought to the attention of President Woodrow Wilson and his cabinet, who reportedly feared reprisals by the German government against Allied POWs for this cold-blooded murder of a German national on American soil.

Other political figures were openly sympathetic to the lynch mob. Idaho senator William Borah cited Prager's lynching as an example of what happens when the law is too lax regarding the suppression of alien subversives such as Prager. Henry Cabot Lodge of Massachusetts, one of the giants of the Senate, suggested that all domestic enemies should be tried and shot by military tribunals.

Newspaper reaction to the lynching was decidedly mixed and reflected varying American attitudes toward the anti-German hysteria that was gripping the nation. While respectable dailies such as the *Chicago Tribune* and the *New York Times* vigorously condemned Prager's murder, the *Grand Rapids Herald* postulated that the kind of mob violence Collinsville had demonstrated might be a necessary evil at a time when conventional American security forces could not safeguard the country from its internal enemies—such as Robert Prager. Astonishingly, the *Washington Post* actually praised the affair as "a healthful awakening in the interior of the country."

Area newspapers viewed the lynching through the lens of bigotry and war hysteria. The *Edwardsville Intelligencer* characterized the lynching as "an unlawful and unjustifiable act" but seemed to assume that Prager was indeed a spy. The United States was at war with Germany, it noted, "and a traitor over there is dealt with summarily." The *St. Louis Globe-Democrat* conveyed its opinion of the event by the headline: "German Enemy of the U.S. Hanged by Mob."

The Collinsville horror undoubtedly inspired an act of violence against an East Alton merchant of German descent. On April 6—just one day after

Prager's lynching—a mob descended on the home of Morris Gotler, who fled to a nearby saloon. The mob pursued Gotler and apprehended him. He was taken to a schoolyard, where he was forced to kiss the flag and engage in similar indignities to prove his loyalty. The mob threatened Gotler with hanging but eventually set him free. Unlike Prager, Gotler was not accused of spying for the Kaiser. His only offense had been neglecting to honor a local merchants' agreement to close his business during a demonstration promoting the sale of liberty bonds.

The Reverend J.D. Metzler, pastor of St. Boniface Catholic Church in Edwardsville, had served his church for more than two decades, but the sixty-three-year-old priest was a German immigrant who had served as an officer in the Kaiser's army. He had angered some of his parishioners by allegedly making pro-German comments and refusing to ring the Angelus according to the federal government's mandated daylight-saving time. On the night following Prager's murder, Metzler was visited by an "Americanization Committee." The next day, the Angelus was rung at 6:00 p.m. rather than 7:00 p.m. Metzler later took a leave of absence from his pulpit, purportedly to avoid a tar-and-feathering.

Repercussions from Prager's lynching extended to the use of the German language. Public schools in Edwardsville, East St. Louis and even St. Louis eliminated instruction in German. The Vigilance Committee of Staunton posted signs throughout the neighborhoods of that town's German community stating that use of the German language had become extremely distasteful to Americans and only English should be spoken in public. Staunton residents who could not speak English were advised to remain silent. Townspeople got the message and spoke only English.

Churches in the Metro East that had traditionally held German-language services switched to English after Prager's lynching. Members of St. Peter's German Lutheran Church in East St. Louis met on April 7 and agreed to drop the word *German* from the official name of their church. The German Methodist Church in Belleville suddenly became the Jackson Street Methodist Church.

The official inquest into Prager's murder was conducted by Roy Lowe, Madison County coroner, from April 8 to April 11, during which time some thirty-three witnesses were heard. Mob ringleader Joseph Riegel made a full confession and implicated four other men: Wesley Beaver, William Brockmeier, Richard Dukes Jr. and Enid Elmore. The findings of a grand jury led to formal charges of murder leveled at twelve men, one of whom—George Davis—could not be located. The men who would stand trial with the original five implicated during the inquest were Calvin Gilmore, John Hallsworth, Cecil Larremore and James de Matties.

The ensuing trial began on May 13. Prosecuting attorneys included Madison County state's attorney J.P. Streuber and two Illinois assistant attorney generals: W.E. Trautmann and C.W. Middlekauf. Thomas Williamson was defense attorney for the accused murderers.

By all accounts, the prosecution made a valiant effort during the three-week trial but to no avail. The almost surreal atmosphere in the courtroom was typified by Riegel's complete repudiation of his earlier confession. He now claimed that he cautioned the crowd to remain calm, touched neither Prager nor the lynch rope and didn't even see the actual lynching until Prager was dangling in the air.

Williamson, in his closing argument for the defense, blatantly stated that the war had developed a new unwritten law that gave patriots, such as the eleven defendants, the right to murder those deemed disloyal to the United States and a threat to national security. Irving Dillard, who attended the trial with his father, noted that a martial band outside the courthouse actually played patriotic tunes within hearing of the jury while Williamson made this impassioned—and frightening—closing statement.

Under these circumstances, it is hardly surprising that the jury took only forty-five minutes—another source claims just twenty-five minutes—to acquit all eleven defendants, a verdict greeted with wild cheers by the crowds within and outside the courtroom. The verdict was ostensibly based on some contradictory evidence and by the fact that Prager's murder had occurred in the dark, thus making it impossible to establish the murderers' identities beyond the shadow of a legal doubt. In all likelihood, Prager's killers would have been acquitted even if the lynching had occurred in broad daylight in the presence of ten thousand witnesses. Just as Prager stood no chance of saving his life on that night of madness, the ringleaders of the mob that lynched him stood no chance of being convicted of his murder.

James O. Monroe, editor and publisher of the *Collinsville Herald*, denounced the trial as "a farcical patriotic orgy account," according to one account. An editorial he wrote after the murderers' acquittal, however, hardly corroborates such a sentiment. Except for "a few persons who may still harbor Germanic inclinations," he stated, "the whole city is glad that the eleven men indicted for the hanging of Robert P. Prager were acquitted." The Collinsville "community is well convinced that he [Prager] was disloyal," and "the city will not miss him." Monroe chillingly suggested that Prager's murder "has a wholesome effect on the Germanists of Collinsville and the rest of the nation."

A member of the Odd Fellows, Prager was buried by that lodge with a small American flag pinned to his chest, just as he had requested, in St. Matthew's Cemetery at Gravois and Bates in South St. Louis. In addition to his name and the dates and places of his birth and death, the tombstone notes that he was "the victim of a mob." No more epitaph is really needed.

The government of Imperial Germany offered to pay Prager's burial expenses, but Governor Lowden announced that the State of Illinois had a moral obligation to pay the bill. The pastor of an Evangelical church conducted the graveside services.

Carl Monroe succeeded his father, James O. Monroe, as publisher and editor of the *Collinsville Herald*. In a 1959 interview, the younger Monroe remarked that Riegel and the other defendants were insignificant figures in the community before the lynching, and most slipped back into obscurity after they were found not guilty. Cecil Larremore, just fifteen at the time of Prager's murder, became the owner of a leading restaurant in Collinsville. Richard "Dick" Dukes Jr. ended up as the town drunk. Monroe also said that Wesley Beaver "didn't do well" but didn't elaborate. The tree from which Prager was hanged—either an elm or a hackberry, depending on which source one consults—was cut down in 1962 amid national media coverage about its infamous role in history. Several Metro East residents kept small pieces of the tree as grim mementos of humanity's periodic inhumanity.

THE KU KLUX KLAN
IN SOUTHWESTERN ILLINOIS

The Ku Klux Klan was formed in Pulaski, Tennessee, on Christmas Eve 1865 by six Confederate Civil War veterans. Nathan Bedford Forrest, a former Confederate general who had served as a slave trader before the Civil War, served as its first Grand Wizard. The KKK quickly spread throughout the South and instituted a reign of terror against the region's newly freed slaves as well as members of the Republican Party, whether Black or white. Confederate veterans, poor white farmers, ex-Democratic politicians and other malcontents costumed themselves in hooded sheets and employed threats, violence and murder to intimidate African Americans from voting, serving on juries, testifying against white people in court, bearing arms and bettering themselves economically. While it is difficult to ascertain a precise number, historians believe that the Klan during this volatile period killed hundreds throughout the South.

The Klan realized that education offered former slaves passage on the road to advancement. Accordingly, it targeted white teachers from the North—many of whom were former abolitionists—who journeyed south to educate Black students in the fundamentals of literacy. These idealistic educators were paid nocturnal visits by Klansmen and warned that their lives would be in jeopardy if they attempted to teach the freed slaves. Many indeed chose to leave the South.

Black southerners and their white allies attempted to resist the KKK, but it became increasingly obvious that federal assistance was needed to curb Klan violence. Congressman Benjamin Franklin Butler of Massachusetts,

Nathan Bedford Forrest, a former Confederate general, was the first Grand Wizard of the Ku Klux Klan. *Public domain, Wikipedia Commons.*

a former Union general, introduced a bill that was signed into law by President Ulysses Grant in 1871. The Ku Klux Klan Act effectively outlawed this white supremacist organization by using federal troops rather than state militias to fight Klan terrorism. Klansmen were prosecuted in federal courts utilizing juries that were predominantly African American. While racist-perpetrated violence against African Americans in the South by no means ceased, the Ku Klux Klan was destroyed.

The Klan's rebirth in 1915, at a mass meeting held at Stone Mountain, Georgia, can be attributed to the phenomenal success of Thomas Dixon's novel *The Clansman: A Historical Romance of the Ku Klux Klan*, published in 1905, and its 1915 film adaptation. Dixon, an ardent white supremacist, portrays Reconstruction as a time when freed slaves, Union soldiers and carpetbagger politicians exploited the defeated South. Virginal white women were routinely raped by African Americans, who are depicted by Dixon as crude and bestial. Heroic young white southerners formed the Ku Klux Klan to redeem their region from the men, white and Black, who sought to destroy it.

While the original KKK never burned crosses, Dixon had them doing so in his novel. This literary innovation proved so popular with readers that the newly reborn Klan adopted the ritual, and the blazing cross quickly became the organization's most recognizable symbol.

The Birth of a Nation proved even more popular than the novel on which it is based. Directed by D.W. Griffith, Dixon's racist vision of the post–Civil War era broke box office records across the United States and was acclaimed a cinematic masterpiece. President Woodrow Wilson, a southerner who had known Dixon when the two were classmates at Johns Hopkins University, watched the film and proclaimed it an accurate depiction of Reconstruction. "My only regret is that it is all so terribly true," Wilson said. Griffith's film succeeded all too well at glamorizing a gang of murderous thugs and selling this image to a large portion of the American public.

While the 1915 version of the Ku Klux Klan loathed African Americans as much as its predecessor, it aimed much of its propaganda at Roman Catholics and Jews. Catholics were portrayed as inherently disloyal Americans who owed their allegiance to the Pope rather than the United States. The Klan accused them of plotting to bring America under the rule of Rome, either through the ballot box or even through armed insurrection. The author remembers his great-uncle, the late Joseph Dromgoole of the *Alton Evening Telegraph*, telling him of a KKK pamphlet warning that stores of firearms were hidden in the basements of Catholic churches for use in this rebellion. My great-uncle said that the author of the pamphlet was obviously not aware that Alton's St. Patrick's Church, to which he belonged, had no basement.

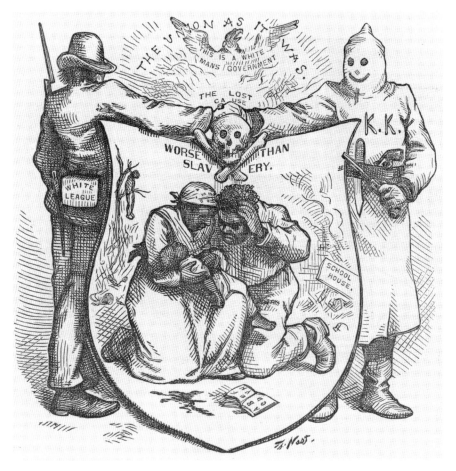

Two members of the Reconstruction-era Ku Klux Klan. *Public domain, courtesy of the Southern Poverty Law Center.*

In addition to Black, Jewish and Catholic Americans, the Klan declared its animosity toward immigrants, "Bolshevism" and those who did not support Prohibition. The white, Anglo-Saxon Protestant was the Klan's paragon. Those who fell short in one or more of these categories could never measure up to this supposed American ideal.

The revived Klan was by no means limited to the South or rural America. The organization was strong in Oregon, virtually ruled Indiana and even established a presence in New England. The Klan flourished in southern cities such as Dallas and Memphis but also gained footholds in Chicago, St. Louis and Detroit. Illinois, a Union state during the Civil War, had ninety-five thousand Klan members, the fifth-largest membership in the nation. East St. Louis had a thriving Klavern, a fact that residents today of that largely Black city find singularly ironic.

Although the East St. Louis Klavern's membership peaked at eight thousand members in 1925, it never succeeded in electing its candidates to municipal office. Black citizens were joined by a coalition of Catholics, Jews and immigrants as well as a number of white Protestants who wanted no part of the Ku Klux Klan. This resistance to the KKK composes a proud chapter in East St. Louis history. Other regions of the country were not so fortunate, however. In 1924, the Klan won almost every race in which it endorsed a candidate. While the organization worked with the Democratic Party in the South, Klansmen frequently supported Republicans in the North and elected GOP governors in Maine, Kansas, Indiana and Colorado. KKK-backed candidates took Senate seats in Kansas, Oklahoma and Colorado.

Precisely when the Ku Klux Klan established itself in Alton remains uncertain. Its original members are all deceased, and their descendants aren't talking. Having a forebear who wore a Klansman's robe and hood isn't the kind of thing that one tends to boast about. Minutes of Klan meetings—if, indeed, minutes were ever taken—either were destroyed long ago or have yet to be located.

It is certain, however, that an Alton Klan was already in existence in 1924 when it purchased for $4,300 the Upper Alton Wesley Chapel. The Methodist congregation that had occupied the building, located at 2014 Main Street, merged with another Methodist church in Upper Alton to form a new Methodist congregation. This church, now known as Main Street United Methodist Church, stands to this day and enjoys the distinction of having counted a young Altonian named Robert Wadlow among its long-ago members. Wadlow (1918–1940) stood 8 feet, 11.1 inches in height and was the tallest human being who ever lived.

The *Alton Evening Telegraph* carried an article in its January 16, 1924 edition that quoted an unnamed Klan "representative," who stated that the organization had acquired the church as a meeting place or "Klavern." Alton's KKK had so many members that it needed a "permanent home," he said. The old Upper Alton Wesley Chapel could hold two hundred, but even that couldn't accommodate all of Alton's Klansmen, the anonymous spokesman insisted. The KKK eventually intended to build an auditorium with an even greater seating capacity, since the Klan would "throw it open for community uses."

The *Telegraph* reporter must have asked about the numerical strength of the Alton Klan, since the article notes that the spokesman declined to say how many members were in the organization. However, he boasted to the reporter that the KKK "had the largest membership of any fraternal organization in the city of Alton." The reporter wrote that, if true, this would place the Klan's membership at over one thousand.

The reporter then observed that the spokesman's response comprised "the nearest statement that has ever been made for publicity as to the membership of the KKK in the Alton chapter." Since this article is the earliest reference to the Ku Klux Klan in the pages of the *Alton Evening Telegraph*, we can surmise two conclusions: Alton's KKK had been in existence for an unknown period of time prior to this article's publication and had consistently resisted giving any indication of its purported strength.

The Klan's choice of Upper Alton, rather than Alton, for its meeting place surprised no one who was familiar with the two cities. Upper Alton was a separate community until 1911, when it was annexed by Alton. The riverside city had a large Catholic population centered on three churches. Saint Mary's Church, in the Middletown district, boasted many German American parishioners, some of whom were quite wealthy. Saint Patrick's Church, located in Alton's Hunterstown neighborhood, had been founded as an ethnic parish for the shanty Irish. Saints Peter and Paul was the See of the Catholic bishop from 1857 to 1923, when Rome transferred the See to Springfield, and the church still lent such a commanding presence to State Street that it was popularly known as Christian Hill. It carries that name to this day, while Saints Peter and Paul is often referred to as the Old Cathedral. Alton's Germans and Irish of the 1920s made no bones about enjoying their beer and whiskey, despite Prohibition.

There were no Catholic churches in Upper Alton. The Baptist, Methodist and Presbyterian denominations held sway. The community also was the site of Shurtleff College, a Northern Baptist school. Drinking had been frowned upon in Upper Alton well before Prohibition went into effect, and the town boasted a thriving chapter of the Woman's Christian Temperance Union. While many Upper Alton residents undoubtedly abhorred the KKK and wanted nothing to do with it, the community's large Protestant population and affinity for Prohibition, which the Klan strongly supported, made the town choice real estate for the Klan.

The Ku Klux Klan next made local headlines when the Reverend J.C. Townsend, pastor of Alton's First Congregational Church, preached a sermon on February 24, 1924, that dealt with the KKK. Those who attended the service expecting a spirited denunciation of the Klan must have been sorely disappointed.

Townsend examined paragraph by paragraph the Klan oath as revised in 1921 and concluded that "if the Klansman lived up to that oath that he would be a better man." The minister voiced one objection to the oath, however—that segment excluding "Negroes, Jews and Catholics" from membership. Townsend stated that he could not subscribe to such discrimination.

He had no quarrel with Catholics, the Congregationalist pastor admonished the crowd. Indeed, he conceded that he would "rather that a man or woman belong to the Catholic Church than to be without the church altogether." Taking a somewhat higher road, Townsend observed that the framers of the U.S. Constitution granted freedom of religion to all Americans and that the offending segment of the Klan oath blatantly flouted that provision.

Townsend then returned to praising the Klan. Calling for "absolute fairness" in discussing the KKK, he said that it was a growing organization "entitled to the strongest praise for the good things in its preamble." With the right kind of leaders, the Klan could accomplish "many good things." Seeking to balance his sermon so as to offend no one, Townsend then returned to decrying religious intolerance and the Klan's exclusion of Catholic, Jewish and Black Americans.

Discrimination against African Americans is an example of discrimination based on race, not religion. According to the *Telegraph* account, however, Townsend took the Klan to task merely for religious discrimination and lumped "Negroes" with Catholics and Jews while making his point. If he deplored the Klan's trademark racism in this sermon, the *Telegraph* reporter failed to note it.

Townsend obviously publicized the topic of this controversial sermon among his fellow Altonians because the *Telegraph* article mentioned that "his audience apparently was made up of both sides"—a statement that indicates

Alton's Klan had an active opposition by this time. The reporter concluded the article with the remark that the opposing sides thought his presentation to be "most fair."

Alton's Klan held its first recorded cross-burning on Friday, June 6, 1924, on the grounds of the old Upper Alton Wesley Chapel. Klansmen in full regalia stood guard on the sidewalks around the church while the cross blazed. The Reverend A.C. Geyer, former pastor of Alton's First Methodist Church who had thrown in with the Klan, served as the keynote speaker.

At Western Military Academy—located disturbingly near Wesley Chapel—Alton's Knights of Columbus, a Catholic fraternal organization, and the Daughters of Isabella, its women's auxiliary, hosted a reception honoring Bishop James Griffin of Springfield. Protestant clergymen and laity were also in attendance, and the WMA auditorium was packed.

While the account of Griffin's address in the *Western Catholic* contained no mention of the Ku Klux Klan or even its cross-burning so nearby, there is little doubt that the event was as much a protest rally as a reception. "There are those who think we are trying to steal the American government and others who think we have designs on the public schools," he said. Griffin denied any such conspiracy among American Catholics, a blunt refutation of Klan charges to the contrary.

He made a strong case for religious toleration. "America has never persecuted religion and it is the best field in the world for brotherly love," he noted. Catholics and non-Catholics in the audience gave Griffin a standing ovation.

The *Alton Evening Telegraph* account of the reception noted that, despite their alarming proximity, there were no physical altercations between the two groups before, during and after the respective gatherings. Joseph Dromgoole, the author's great-uncle who attended Griffin's reception at WMA, characterized the event to the author as "our answer to the Klan and its bigotry."

Ironically, the Klan's next major public spectacle was the funeral of one of its more prominent members. On his deathbed, Harry Lessner requested that the formal ritual of the Ku Klux Klan be performed at his burial.

Lessner's membership in the organization underscores the Klan's appeal to citizens of good repute. A former glassblower, Lessner was elected a police magistrate in 1911 and, later, won the office of justice of the peace. He had also served on the Alton City Council and the city's board of education. The Upper Alton resident had been a member of the Modern Woodmen and the Knights of Pythias.

Harry Lessner was laid to rest after his fellow Klan members performed a secret ritual at his grave.

It was Lessner's desire to be buried on a Sunday. Klan members placed a telephone call to Alton mayor George T. Davis while he was attending church to request that Klansmen be allowed to wear their hoods during the funeral procession to Oakwood Cemetery in Upper Alton. Davis declined, citing a 1923 state law that prohibited anyone in a public parade from wearing a mask. The measure, which had been signed by Illinois governor Len Small, had been specifically passed by the legislature to prevent the KKK from parading in robes and hoods. The measure also provided for lengthy sentences for those who committed crimes while wearing masks of any kind.

Lessner's funeral at the Klavern drew several thousand mourners, Klan and non-Klan. The service was conducted by the Reverend S.D. McKenney, pastor of Alton's Cherry Street Baptist Church.

Word had spread throughout town that the KKK intended to march to the grave site in full apparel. Motorists eager to view the exotic spectacle lined the procession route until every parking space was taken. The robed Klansmen indeed observed the mayor's demand that their hoods must be raised. Women Klan members, however, feared recognition by onlookers more than Mayor Davis's wrath and wore hoods to conceal their faces. There is no indication that they were prosecuted for blatantly flouting state law. When the procession finally ended at Lessner's grave, the Klansmen dropped their hoods, content that the letter of the law had been observed.

While an estimated 170 Klansmen and women participated in the funeral procession, this was a far cry from more than 1,000 members claimed by the Klan spokesman in January 1924. Newspaper reporters and anti-Klan activists noted that Alton's Klavern must be fewer than the modest number of 170. Many of the Klansmen's automobile license plates indicated that they resided in Madison County communities other than Alton. A number hailed from the East St. Louis Klavern.

An *Alton Evening Telegraph* photo shows a cluster of hooded, white-robed figures encircling Lessner's grave. The KKK in turn is surrounded by a large number of onlookers who might be non-Klan mourners or—more likely—the simply curious. There is no known account of precisely what the Klan's graveside ritual involved.

Lessner's funeral marked the Klan's last foray into the pages of Alton's newspaper. There are no records of additional cross-burnings or funeral processions. Never numerically large, despite its claims to the contrary, Alton's Klan entered a period of decline. Why? Part of the reason can be found in the negative publicity that had begun to engulf the Klan around the nation.

David Stephenson, KKK Grand Dragon of Indiana and several other states, enjoyed such power in the Hoosier State that he often boasted that "I am the law in Indiana." In 1925—the same year as Lessner's celebrated KKK funeral—he kidnapped Madge Oberholtzer, a young schoolteacher, and brutally raped her in his private train car. Imprisoned by Stephenson in an Indiana hotel room, Oberholtzer attempted suicide by swallowing mercuric chloride tablets. When he discovered her vomiting blood, Stephenson drove her home and dropped her off.

Oberholtzer died of mercury poisoning but not before relating the horror she had endured from Stephenson's attack. The Grand Dragon, virtually a dictator in Indiana, had bitten the young woman so badly that an attending physician stated that it looked as though she had been attacked by a pack of wolves. One of her nipples literally had been bitten off.

Stephenson soon discovered that he was not the law in Indiana. He was convicted of second-degree murder and sentenced to life in prison, although he was paroled in 1950.

The 1920s Ku Klux Klan, which so often publicized itself as the defender of "womanhood" and Christian morality, was devastated by the scandal. Klan members across the nation resigned in droves. The KKK strongly supported Prohibition, a position that sat well with "dry" Americans who otherwise differed with the Klan on social issues. The fact that Stephenson had plied Oberholtzer with alcohol before the attack further humiliated the organization.

Several incidents in Alabama also helped to undermine the KKK. In their campaign to enforce what they perceived as morality, Klansmen kidnapped a divorced woman, stripped her to the waist and then whipped the woman after tying her to a tree. Other flogging victims included a naturalized American citizen who had married a native-born woman and a Black man who had refused to sell his land. Grover Cleveland Hall Sr., editor of the *Montgomery (AL) Advertiser*, won a Pulitzer Prize for a series of editorials attacking the Klan. That such a thing could occur in Dixie underscored the Klan's collapsing support.

The KKK, which had boasted a national membership of six million in 1924, was so weakened by 1928 that it was powerless to prevent New York governor Al Smith, an Irish Catholic, from winning the Democratic Party's presidential nomination. To add insult to injury, Smith lost the general election but carried the Deep South that so idolized the post–Civil War Ku Klux Klan. By the 1930s, the Klan was a shadow of its former self. A few fanatics kept it alive, but the final blow came in 1944 when the IRS filed a lien against the Klan for $685,000 in back taxes. The Grand Wizard then formally dissolved the organization, although some Klaverns simply went underground.

The Ku Klux Klan was reborn yet again in the 1950s as a result of racist opposition to the civil rights movement. Today, however, it is a mistake to speak of a Ku Klux Klan, since there are any number of KKK factions, each claiming to be the true successor of the Reconstruction Klan as romanticized in Dixon's novel and Griffith's film. The contemporary Ku Klux Klan groups rail against African Americans, Jews, immigrants, communists and liberals but generally are less inclined to demonize Catholics than the 1920s Klan.

The Ku Klux Klan enjoyed a brief resurgence in southwestern Illinois during the last decade of the twentieth century. The Klan engaged in a period of anonymous proselytizing in 1992 by leaving fliers in yards and even businesses. I recall an Alton supermarket employee who was distinctly nonplussed at finding a stack of Klan flyers on a shelf of canned goods. Sometime later, the Knights of the Ku Klux Klan, one of the most active Klan factions at the time, announced that a cross-burning would be held on September 12, 1992, at the residence of Ku Klux Klan member Terry Taviner on the 3900 block of Torch Club Road in Fosterburg.

Grand Wizard Thom Robb of Harrison, Arkansas, and other speakers harangued about two hundred Klansmen and their supporters for two and a half hours, beginning at 7:00 p.m. Standing on a porch while addressing a crowd that included women and children, Robb stated, "The white population will be less than 50 percent in less than sixty years." Seeking to frighten his audience even further, he warned, "If you think you have trouble with minorities today, what will it be like when they are the majority?" At approximately 9:30 p.m., the cross was set ablaze.

About forty protesters from Southern Illinois University at Edwardsville (SIUE), who had been organized by the late Dr. John Broyer of the philosophy department, held a protest in front of Taviner's home. The protesters and Klan supporters were separated by about thirty Madison County sheriff's deputies, who were assisted by members of the Illinois State Police and the Alton Police Department.

The opposing groups frequently got into shouting matches. One SIUE protester pointed to a Klan supporter and asked him why he was wearing a Michael Jordan T-shirt if he really believed in white supremacy. The Klan supporter immediately removed the T-shirt and put it on inside-out so that Jordan's image was no longer visible.

A different kind of anti-Klan protest was held on Alton's Lincoln-Douglas Square that evening. Community activists organized a Unity Rally to affirm the commitment of southwestern Illinois residents to justice and equality. An estimated three hundred people attended the Unity Rally, which drew a number of students from Principia College in Elsah and McKendree College in Lebanon. Speakers included civil rights activist Josephine Beckwith, Assistant State's Attorney Duane Bailey, Godfrey's Temple Israel president David Davison and several others.

There was no physical interaction between Klan supporters and Unity Rally participants. However, the author remembers cars driven down East Broadway whose occupants yelled "White power!" at us.

Although Robb pronounced the Fosterburg cross-burning a resounding success, at least one professional researcher begged to differ. Larry Powell, a photojournalist from Western Kentucky University who had trailed the Klan for five years, said that an attendance of two hundred at the cross-burning couldn't be construed as an accurate reflection of Klan strength in the River Bend. "Most of the people were gawkers," he said. Powell estimated that only about sixty members of the crowd were actually Klansmen.

He postulated that the actual Klan presence in southwestern Illinois was quite small. Most of the Klansmen at the cross-burning were wearing patches from states other than Illinois, Powell observed.

The next attempt by the Knights of the Ku Klux Klan to build a base in southwestern Illinois occurred in Edwardsville, the seat of Madison County, when the organization held a rally on the plaza between the county courthouse and the administration building on May 6, 1994. The event was organized by Klan leader Basil Sitzes Sr. of Cottage Hills and billed as a protest against the national holiday in honor of Dr. Martin Luther King Jr.

Christine McGiffen, one of only two women present and wife of Illinois Klan coordinator Dennis McGiffen, opened the rally by welcoming "all white brothers and sisters." McGiffen was followed by Dave Newman, Michigan Klan coordinator, and Troy Murphy, Indiana Klan coordinator. Thom Robb then delivered his address.

The rally lasted only sixty-five minutes and drew just forty Klansmen, most of whom wore white shirts, ties and black pants rather than sheets. Over one hundred state, county and local law enforcement officers, many of them in riot gear, separated Klan supporters from about three hundred jeering protesters. One Edwardsville resident hired a musician to play the bagpipes while Klan speakers attempted to address the crowd. Klan members occasionally shouted back at the protesters and taunted them by extending their arms in Nazi-like salutes whenever Robb lambasted traditional Klan targets on the basis of their race, religion, ethnic origin and sexual orientation.

Taking a cue from Alton's 1992 Unity Rally, Edwardsville activists organized a protest march designated as a "Walk of Commitment." The march began at the Edwardsville Sports Complex and ended one mile away on the grounds of the ESIC Baptist Church, where a rally was held. The author remembers marchers being cautioned not to respond to jeers or other forms of harassment from any KKK sympathizers we encountered. Police cars accompanied us along the march. We were not harassed in any way.

Speakers at the rally extolled the importance of working to build a just, compassionate society in which bigotry had no place. Edwardsville resident Ana Brown read a letter from Oscar Arias of Costa Rica, winner of the 1987 Nobel Peace Prize, that deplored the Klan's rally and stressed the importance of diversity. "When diversity generates unity," Arias's letter stated, "a most beautiful picture emerges." Edwardsville mayor Gary Niebur told the crowd, "Today, we have been forced to host some most unwelcome guests—hatred and bigotry." Niebur left no doubt in the minds of the rally's participants and listeners regarding his attitude toward the Klan. "We will neither welcome nor will we abide such visitors in our community."

While there are undoubtedly Klan members in the River Bend as of this writing, the organization hasn't sponsored any further cross-burnings or rallies. Area residents who participated in the anti-Klan protests will always take pride for having stood up for human rights.

The old Upper Alton Wesley Chapel that once served as the Klavern of Alton's Ku Klux Klan still stands on Main Street. It has had many occupants over the years, including a church that was a member of a historically Black denomination. Those long-dead Klansmen surely turned over in their graves.

JAMES EARL RAY AND THE MURDER OF DR. MARTIN LUTHER KING JR.

The confessed assassin of Dr. Martin Luther King Jr. was born on March 10, 1928, in his family's house at 1021 West Ninth Street in what was then the red-light district of my hometown of Alton. The residence has since been torn down, and the lot remains empty. Ray later referred to the neighborhood as a place so rough that the toughest characters in the fiction of Mark Twain would have been considered sissies. He was the eldest of ten children born to parents who never escaped from the cycle of poverty.

Ray claimed his family was nominally Catholic and that in 1934 his parents enrolled him in the first grade of St. Mary's School, located on the corner of East Third and Henry Streets. He was forced to leave St. Mary's before the academic year ended when his father was run out of Alton because of his involvement in a forgery scheme. The Ray family moved to Quincy, Illinois, in 1935 and finally settled in a rundown farmhouse outside Ewing, Missouri, across the Mississippi River from Quincy.

James Earl Ray's first altercation with the law occurred in 1942 when the fourteen-year-old was visiting his grandmother in Alton. Ray grabbed a bundle of newspapers that had been tossed from a delivery truck and began selling the papers himself. The police seized the young thief and ended Ray's entrepreneurial enterprise.

The Ray family moved to Galesburg, Illinois, but James decided to live with his grandmother in Alton. He dropped out of school at sixteen and took a job in 1944 as a laborer at the old International Shoe Tannery in Hartford, Illinois. When World War II ended and the military cut back its orders,

James Earl Ray claimed that he briefly attended St. Mary's Catholic School in Alton.

however, Ray was laid off. With no high school diploma or marketable skills, his job outlook was poor. An army recruiter in East St. Louis persuaded Ray to enlist.

Ray was sent to Germany but received a general discharge in 1948 for what the army termed "ineptness." Ray returned to Alton and then decided to hit the road. He moved to Chicago, then drifted west to Los Angeles. He visited his family, now living in Quincy's seedy riverfront area, and then returned to Chicago. It was during this aimless period of his life that Ray acquired his first arrest as an adult: April 18, 1950, on a vagrancy charge in Cedar Rapids, Iowa.

But it was in the Windy City that Ray's life of crime began in earnest. His bungling as a criminal, however, easily rivaled his incompetence as a soldier. Fleeing from Chicago police after robbing a cab driver of eleven dollars, Ray raced into a dead-end alley where a cop's bullet passed through both his arms. Ray fell through a basement window and cut open his face. This botched caper earned him a stretch at the state prison in Joliet and the state prison farm at Pontiac from 1952 to 1954. Upon his release, Ray returned to the River Bend to ply his criminal trade. On October 28, 1954, the hapless Ray was arrested for the burglary of the National Cleaners in East Alton. Ray had jumped through a plate-glass window, losing his loafers and badly cutting his feet. When the police arrived, they disabled Ray's getaway car. He walked miles to a relative's house, where he was shortly apprehended by the police, who simply followed his bloody footprints.

Ray was indicted for the National Cleaners burglary, but the case never went to trial. While out on bail, Ray was arrested for breaking and entering a U.S. Post Office in Hannibal, Missouri. He was sentenced to three years and nine months in the federal prison at Leavenworth, Kansas.

In 1958, Ray's father deserted his wife for another woman and moved to the Soulard area of St. Louis. Ray's mother and some of his siblings chose to settle in Soulard as well. Upon release from prison, Ray also moved to St. Louis and then returned to Alton to resume his criminal activity. He robbed two grocery stores in the Gateway City and then robbed Wegener's, a grocery store located on the corner of Alby and East Ninth Streets in Alton.

Store owner Mary Wegener told a *Life* magazine reporter in 1968 that she initially thought it was some kind of bizarre joke. "At first, I thought he was fooling around so I started telling him about God and then he pulled the gun." Wegener recalled Ray's behavior as erratic. "He chased people all around the store. He just ran around like a wild man." Nine years after the robbery, Wegener admitted, "I can still feel his gun in my back." The author's grandmother, who lived next door to Wegener's, was shopping for groceries in the store at the time of the robbery.

This Alton grocery store was known as Wegener's when it was robbed by James Earl Ray during one of his local crime sprees.

A police officer on a three-wheel motorcycle chased Ray and an accomplice as they fled the scene in their car. Ray jumped from the vehicle and escaped, but his cohort was captured after stopping the car and fleeing into some woods. Police found firearms that had been used in the robbery in the getaway car. Convicted of the St. Louis robberies, Ray was sentenced to serve twenty years at the Missouri State Penitentiary, which he entered in March 1960.

He escaped in April 1967 and shortly met with two of his brothers in Chicago. Authorities believe that James Earl Ray and another man robbed the Bank of Alton on July 13, 1967. Armed with a shotgun, the pair scooped up $30,000 from the cash drawers. Police found the partially burned shoulder stock for a shotgun and clothing worn by the robbers near a street where Ray's relatives lived in Alton. The day after the Alton robbery, Ray paid cash for a car in East St. Louis. Investigators also believe that Ray used money from the bank robbery to purchase the 30.06 Remington Gamemaster hunting rifle that he used to assassinate King.

The U.S. House Select Committee on Assassinations concluded in 1978 that Ray killed the civil rights leader in order to earn a $50,000 bounty that had been placed on King's head some years earlier by a clique of white supremacists. Conrad "Pete" Baetz of Glen Carbon, a former Madison County sheriff's deputy who served as an investigator for the committee, stated in an exclusive interview with the *Telegraph* that the conspirators met in a home on Arsenal Street in St. Louis. The site, according to Baetz, was about two hundred yards from the Grapevine Tavern, which was owned by Ray's brother John Ray.

Ray learned about the bounty while he was on the run or possibly while he was still in the Missouri State Penitentiary. He began stalking King as the civil rights figure traveled around the nation. Ray caught up with King in Memphis, where the Nobel Prize winner was trying to bolster support for striking sanitation workers. Ray checked into a boardinghouse across from the Lorraine Motel, where King was staying. He fired his rifle from the bathroom window and killed King with a single bullet to his throat while the revered civil rights activist was standing on the balcony of his motel.

Ray dropped the rifle, which carried his fingerprints, outside the motel, as well as a portable radio that had been inscribed with his prisoner number while he was incarcerated at the Missouri State Penitentiary. Using money garnered from the Bank of Alton robbery, Ray fled to Canada and then, with the aid of a fake passport, to London. Baetz stated that Ray intended to go to Africa and seek employment as a mercenary.

Ray was apprehended at London's Heathrow Airport in June 1968. At the time of his arrest, he had only $123 in his pocket. Baetz is not certain whether Ray ever received the $50,000 bounty that had been offered by the white supremacists.

Southwestern Illinois residents were shocked to learn that King's assassin was a native of their region. The national media reporters who descended on Alton to learn more about Ray found any number of people who were willing to talk. Alton police chief William Peterson described Ray as "the kind of criminal who gets into all kinds of trouble, hates and has no respect for the law." William Maher, an uncle of James Earl Ray, dismissed him as "the kind of guy who only turned up when he wanted something—like bail money." He also remarked that "every time he came back here, he got into trouble."

In March 1969, Ray pleaded guilty and was sentenced to ninety-nine years in prison. He soon recanted and, for the rest of his life, insisted that he had not killed King. In a crudely written 1988 autobiography, Ray insisted that he was framed by a man called Raoul. Ray claimed that Raoul, a mysterious figure he had met in Montreal after escaping from the Missouri State Penitentiary, took a rifle the two of them had purchased in Alabama to show to dealers in Memphis.

On the day of King's assassination, according to Ray, he went to see Raoul at the boardinghouse across the street from the Lorraine Motel, but Raoul turned him away. He later heard about the assassination on the radio of his white Mustang and fled when he heard they were looking for a white man who was driving such a vehicle. Raoul, Ray argued, must have deliberately left the rifle, which contained the former Altonian's fingerprints, at the crime scene to implicate him. Baetz and other authorities believe that Raoul is a product of Ray's imagination. Anna Sandhu, a courtroom artist who was married to Ray from 1978 to 1992 while he was in prison, initially believed that Ray was innocent but later became convinced of his guilt.

As the one generally acknowledged to be King's killer, Ray was not popular with some of the Black inmates at Brushy Mountain State Prison in Petros, Tennessee, where he served his sentence. He was assaulted by three Black inmates in 1980 while using the prison's law library. Ray was stabbed in the arm, face and chest.

Ray died on April 23, 1998, of liver disease from a blood transfusion he received in prison. He never stopped protesting his innocence and gained some unlikely supporters. A year before his death, Ray was visited in prison by Dexter King, a son of Dr. Martin Luther King Jr. He told King that he had nothing to do with his father's death. King replied that he believed him. A few days later, Martin Luther King III, Dexter King's older brother, announced that he also believed Ray to be innocent and that the former Altonian had been framed as a patsy by conspirators.

Ray's funeral was held at Metropolitan Interdenominational Church, a prominent Black church in Nashville. Coretta Scott King declined an invitation to attend the service, although she sent a note of consolation to the Ray family.

Jerry Ray secretly scattered his brother's ashes in Ireland, the nation of the family's ancestors. While James Earl Ray's mother and grandmother are buried in a local cemetery, James had no desire to be buried in the Alton area. Jerry Ray explained that his brother was afraid that his remains would be dug up by a prankster.

The author drove by the vacant lot in Alton where the Ray home formerly stood for about two weeks after Ray's death. I felt it was my duty as a member of the Alton Human Relations Commission to see whether anyone placed a memorial bouquet on the lot and, if so, to remove it.

Fortunately, racists were either too apathetic to care about Ray's death or too stupid to find the lot. No bouquets showed up. The only flowers that have ever been visible at the birthplace of James Earl Ray are dandelions.

THE NIKE MISSILE BASE
AT PERE MARQUETTE STATE PARK

Pere Marquette State Park, located just outside of Grafton in Jersey County, well deserves its reputation as one of the most beautiful state parks in Illinois. Built by the Civilian Conservation Corps in the 1930s, its six thousand acres feature several hiking trails that lead to McAdams Peak, a lookout point with a truly awe-inspiring view of deep woods as well as the Illinois River that flows past the park. Even the briefest sojourn at Pere Marquette Park infuses visitors with the kind of peace and tranquility that only nature can impart.

It seems beyond belief that a place of such breathtaking beauty played a vital role in our nation's Cold War struggle with the Soviet Union. Yet, such was the case.

From 1960 to 1968, Pere Marquette State Park was the site of a Nike missile base that was capable of shooting down any enemy aircraft that menaced St. Louis, Missouri and southwestern Illinois. The motto of U.S. Army personnel who staffed Nike bases across the United States was "If it flies, it dies." The men who served at these bases will attest that this was not an empty slogan.

The Nike missile saga began at the conclusion of World War II when the U.S. Army realized that conventional antiaircraft artillery would be ineffective against jet aircraft. In 1945, Bell Telephone Laboratories issued a paper titled "Anti-Aircraft Guided Missile Report" that envisioned a two-stage supersonic missile that could be guided to its target by a ground-based radar and computer system.

Projectiles fired by antiaircraft artillery follow a predetermined ballistic trajectory that can't be altered after firing. The course of a guided missile, on the other hand, can be altered from ground control so that it finds its target, regardless of any evasive action taken by the pilot of the enemy aircraft. The program for the development and deployment of the U.S. Army's guided missile program was named Nike, after the Greek goddess of victory. The world's first successful guided missile program, it rendered antiaircraft artillery obsolete.

The Nike program acquired critical importance in 1949 when the Soviet Union exploded its first atomic bomb. Washington and the Pentagon worried that the USSR might construct a fleet of long-range bombers that could rain nuclear weapons on major U.S. population areas as well as strategically important targets. The outbreak of the Korean War in 1950 provided further impetus to develop the Nike program and get it in place.

Nike missile bases were charged with the mission of providing a last-ditch line of defense for selected areas. These antiaircraft missiles were to be launched in the event that the long-range fighter-interceptor aircraft of the U.S. Air Force failed to destroy enemy aircraft. Accordingly, Nike bases were constructed in defensive rings surrounding major urban and industrial areas. Some missile sites were located on government land, such as military bases. Others, however, were built on land that had to be acquired from reluctant owners. The federal government often had to go to court in order to obtain the necessary property. Ultimately, about 250 missile bases were built across the continental United States during the 1950s and early 1960s.

The first Nike missile was successfully test-fired in 1951. This missile, the Ajax model, was a two-staged guided missile that reached a maximum speed of 1,600 miles per hour and could destroy a target at altitudes up to 70,000 feet. The Ajax was armed with three high-explosive, fragmentation-type warheads located at the front, center and rear of its missile body.

But the Ajax possessed a serious drawback that could have proven fatal to the United States in the event of an enemy attack. Its effective range was only twenty-five miles. The army seriously considered compensating for this liability by arming the Ajax with a nuclear warhead. Instead, it was decided to build another missile that had a greater range—as well as the capacity to carry a nuclear warhead.

The Hercules missile, successor to the Ajax, possessed a maximum range of about 90 miles and reached a top speed in excess of 2,700 miles per hour. It could destroy a target at an altitude of 150,000 feet, which

The Nike Hercules missile was designed to shoot down enemy aircraft. *Public domain.*

was over twice that of its predecessor. Like the Ajax, the Hercules could be equipped with a high-explosive, fragmentation-type warhead, which was designated T-45. Still, it was its nuclear warhead that made the Hercules such a tremendously lethal weapon.

The atomic bomb dropped on Hiroshima had a yield of approximately fifteen kilotons. The Hercules nuclear warhead, designated W-31, was available in three yields: a three-Kiloton low yield, a twenty-Kiloton medium yield and a thirty-Kiloton high yield. A single W-31 warhead stood capable of annihilating a closely spaced formation of enemy aircraft in addition to destroying any nuclear weapons aboard those aircraft.

The Hercules was a surface-to-surface missile as well. Deployed within western Europe, it would have been used in the event of war to destroy concentrations of enemy troops, armored vehicles, bridges and dams.

Hercules missiles located on the coasts of the continental United States would have been fired against enemy ships and submarines.

The army's decision to build a Nike missile base in southwestern Illinois should have surprised no one. In addition to providing that "last ditch" defense for a relatively large population, the area contained industries that would have proven critical during a war. East Alton is home to the Olin Corporation, while Wood River, Hartford and Roxana contain oil refineries. McDonnell-Douglas and Boeing in neighboring St. Louis produced aircraft. Southwestern Illinois and St. Louis might well have been priority targets if the USSR had gone to war with the United States.

While locating a missile base here might have been a logical choice, it was also a controversial choice. Area residents treasured Pere Marquette State Park, and some worried that the construction of a Nike missile base would destroy its beauty and place much of the park off-limits to the public. A conservation-minded couple who lived on Levis Lane in Godfrey wrote and distributed a pamphlet in 1959, while construction of the base was still in progress, that contended Pere Marquette Park was being ruined.

The pamphlet claimed 95 percent of the park was now closed to the public, and an estimated fifty acres of the park had been devastated beyond recognition. Homer Studebaker, park superintendent, and A.A. Ostermier of the U.S. Army Corps of Engineers denied the charges. Studebaker insisted that the base wouldn't interfere with the public's use of Pere Marquette State Park and camping would resume on schedule in June 1959.

Ostermier, speaking for the Chicago District of the Corps of Engineers, which was building the base, told the *Alton Evening Telegraph* that the base would cover only about twenty-five acres. This figure, according to Ostermier, included six acres for the control area, nine acres to provide housing for staff and ten acres that would be used for the launching area. Philip Pusateri, resident engineer in charge of construction, stated that the base should be completed in May 1959, although installation of the missile-launching mechanism would take longer.

The environmentalist couple printed and distributed several thousand copies of their pamphlet to warn area residents about the purported threat to Pere Marquette State Park posed by the Nike base. To no one's surprise, however, the U.S. Army prevailed. Southwestern Illinois got its Nike base.

Lieutenant Robert G. Smits, acting commanding officer of the base, announced on Friday, July 17, that between 10 and 15 men were scheduled to arrive on July 20 to begin operations at the site. The men would serve as administrative personnel, he noted. Smits stated that the base's full

The dilapidated sentry box outside the fenced-off entrance to the Nike base.

complement would be approximately 110 men—over 90 enlisted men and 8 officers. He expected the base to be at full strength by October.

Smits conceded that only the administrative section of the base had been completed. This section included the barracks as well as the personnel headquarters. Like Ostermier, he noted that the base contained three sections, although he designated them somewhat differently. According to Smits, they were the administrative area, launching area and fire-control area. There were three launching sites, and each site was capable of firing four missiles. The fire-control area, situated two miles from the rest of the site on the highest point of ground in the park, consisted of three types of radar that located and tracked the target and then tracked the missile fired at that target.

The army realized that many area residents were extremely apprehensive about having a Nike missile base in their collective backyard. Smits attempted to allay their fears by stating that there would be no test firing of the missiles. Drills conducted at the base would incorporate only a mock preparation for a launching. The Hercules missiles would not be launched, except in the event of an enemy attack during wartime, Smits insisted.

The base became fully operational and formally began its active service in May 1960. Area residents gradually accepted its presence in Grafton as part of the natural order of things, while some even welcomed its location in their midst. After all, these folks reasoned, Nike missiles were intended to be a last-ditch line of defense for specific American regions, and this vicinity was fortunate indeed to have been selected as such a region.

The author recalls a conversation with an area couple who told him about some local residents who went to Pere Marquette State Park during the Cuban Missile Crisis in 1962, when it seemed that war between the United States and the USSR was a terrifyingly real possibility. These residents evidently believed that, should the Soviet Union attack our country, the Nike base made the park one of the safest places to be. The couple quoted one of those residents as saying that, before everything was destroyed in a nuclear war, he at least wanted to see those missiles fired since it surely would be a grand sight.

The world's two superpowers almost going to war and the role this military installation might have played in such a conflict gave area residents a keen appreciation of the base's importance in our nation's defense. What once had been regarded as a simple curiosity or an environmental catastrophe in a much-beloved state park was now regarded as a vital component of the community and even a source of pride. Some residents took to boasting to out-of-town relatives and friends about the base's presence.

This pride was further enhanced when the base acquired a reputation for excellence in 1965. Lieutenant General Charles B. Duff, commanding general of the Army Air Defense Command, presented the Robert Ward Berry Memorial Award to D Battery of the First Missile Battalion, which staffed the base, for demonstrating the highest degree of proficiency in the Army Air Defense Command annual technical proficiency inspection, short-notice annual practice and maintenance-management inspection. The battery's score for short-notice firing—referred to as a "snap" score— was 98.7, Duff noted in his address. The battery's readiness evaluation was equally outstanding, he said.

Lieutenant John G. Meiger, battery commander, accepted the award on behalf of D Battery. Other military figures at the presentation ceremony included Brigadier General H.E. Michelet of the Army Air Defense Command; Colonel Frank Bates, St. Louis area defense commander; Colonel James L. McGarvey, commander of the First Missile Battalion; and Captain John Leach and Lieutenant Elton P. Ahauf, both former commanders of D Battery.

The *Alton Evening Telegraph* included the missile base in a 1965 series of articles about people who worked on Christmas. An army private, designated the vanguard, always occupied the ready room on the base. The vanguard on Christmas of 1965 was Ollie C. Dalton. The article noted that, even when other personnel were enjoying a special Christmas dinner, Dalton would be seated alone in the fire-control area as he monitored the all-important radar screen. The person closest to Dalton during his lonely vigil would be a sergeant in a room that connected with the ready room by a long hallway. This sergeant, the feature observed, would be able to see other personnel and carry on conversations—but not Dalton.

Dalton told the reporter that his parents and six siblings lived in Reynolds Station, Kentucky, which was about three hundred miles from the base. But he hadn't even bothered to apply for Christmas leave because "I knew somebody had to stay." Dalton's patriotism didn't entirely preclude homesickness, however. "Maybe I can get home right after Christmas," he told the reporter.

The army recognized the importance of cultivating the goodwill of the local population. Consequently, the Marquette Park base occasionally held open houses that allowed the public to tour selected areas of the installation. One such open house occurred from noon to 4:00 p.m. on Armed Forces Day 1967. The event drew a sizable crowd of single adults, parents with children and veterans from all branches of the military.

It's important to realize that this open house occurred during the Vietnam War, America's most controversial conflict. Antiwar rallies were flaring up across the country, and military installations were frequently picketed by protesters. This Nike base had become such a source of pride for area residents, however, that it could host a well-attended open house with nary a protester in sight. That era's hostility toward all things military—a hostility that would play a decisive role in closing Alton's Western Military Academy in 1971—did not touch the Nike base.

Then again, perhaps the base would have been affected by America's anti-military bias if it had remained operational a bit longer. Just one year after hosting that open house, however, the Nike base was closed.

By the late 1950s and early 1960s, the USSR realized that manned aircraft sent to bomb the United States would be overwhelmed by American interceptor aircraft armed with rockets and missiles. The few Soviet bombers that managed to elude these aircraft would be destroyed by missiles fired from Nike bases, such as the one at Marquette Park. The Kremlin decided that the Soviet Union should devote its resources toward

The Nike base at Marquette State Park in Grafton is long gone, but the road leading to it still exists.

developing Intercontinental Ballistic Missiles (ICBMs), against which there was no effective defense at the time.

Aircraft bombers still played a crucial role in warfare. Indeed, when the Marquette Park base was closed in 1968, the United States was bombing North Vietnam. But the era of the intercontinental aircraft bomber was over. America's Nike bases with their Hercules missiles were no longer vital to our nation's defense. By 1974, every Nike base had been closed.

All military equipment was removed from Marquette Park's Nike base by 1969, and the land once occupied by the site was again in possession of the park. The base's buildings were made available for park use, although they remained on army inventory until about 1990. At that time, ownership of the buildings was formally transferred to the State of Illinois.

The old Nike site became a destination for adventurous young people who wanted to explore the area. Scaling the fence that surrounded the main entrance or finding other ways to enter the base rivaled hiking the park's trails in popularity. Humorous tales abound regarding this phase of the base's history. The author recalls an area resident's story about exploring the site with a friend one night. The two companions discovered some teenyboppers and decided to give them a fright. The area resident's friend focused the beam of his huge flashlight on the teenage trespassers while bellowing, "This is the military police! You are all under arrest for trespassing on a restricted military area! Remain where you are until further instructed!" The panic-stricken teenyboppers fled in all directions.

The old base was the scene of a major demolition operation in 1993. Independent contractors removed the hydraulic lifts that raised and lowered the thirty-foot missiles, demolished the silos and then filled them with gravel. Terry Widman, whose father had helped construct the site, noted that the walls in each control room were two and a half feet thick with watertight doors weighing about five tons each. "We demolished them all," he said. Widman referred to Missile Silo No. 3 as a "dinosaur grave" and remarked that his team had worked almost seventy hours a week for three weeks to fill in the three huge silos with gravel.

Visitors to Marquette Park today can see the dilapidated sentry box at the old site's entrance. According to Richard Niemeyer, director of natural resources for Marquette Park, a few buildings yet remain beyond the fence that encloses the site. One of the barracks was spared demolition. In the silo area, a gutted building that formerly contained the generator remains. Four or five gutted buildings that housed radar equipment still stood when I last visited the site.

Perhaps this section of the park will someday be opened to the public. Visitors with a knowledge of history will ponder the irony of picnicking on grounds that once harbored nuclear weapons while dedicated servicemen watched the sky for Soviet aircraft.

BIBLIOGRAPHY

The Wood River Massacre

Alton (IL) Evening Telegraph. "Large Crowd at Monument Dedication." September 12, 1910.

———. "Monument to the Wood River Massacre." August 23, 1910.

Alton (IL) Telegraph. "Revolutionary War Vets Honored." December 14, 2007.

Dunphy, John J. "The Moores of Madison County: A Pioneer and Civil War Saga." *Springhouse Magazine,* 2019.

Emery, Tom. "Wood River Massacre Was a Bloody Event in War of 1812." *AdVantage,* August 20, 2019.

History of Madison County, Illinois. Illustrated with Biographical Sketches of Many Prominent Men and Pioneers. Edwardsville, IL: W.R. Brink and Company, 1882.

Huber, Don. "There's Another Head Stone." *Alton (IL) Telegraph,* February 25, 2007.

Jung, Katherine. "Museum Gets Second Massacre Stone." *Alton (IL) Telegraph,* April 21, 2007.

Massey, Kay Stobbs. "Kay (Stobbs) Massey's Story of the 2nd Moore Stone." Unpublished paper housed in the archives of the Alton Museum of History and Art.

Norton, W.T., ed. *Centennial History of Madison County, Illinois and Its People, 1812–1912.* Chicago: Lewis Publishing Company, 1912.

Portraits and Biographical Record of Madison County, Illinois—Containing Biographical Sketches of Prominent and Representative Citizens of the County, Together with

Biographies and Portraits of All the Presidents of the United States. Chicago: Biographical Publishing Company, 1894.

The Mystery of Jean Lafitte's Grave

Arthur, Stanley Clisby. *Jean Laffite, Gentleman Rover.* New Orleans, LA: Harmanson, 1952.

Asbury, Herbert. *The French Quarter: An Informal History of the French Underworld.* New York: Garden City Publishing Company, 1938.

Brookkhiser, Richard. "Conscientious Objectors." *Time,* March 26, 2007.

Dunphy, John J. "Is Jean Lafitte Buried in Alton?" *Springhouse Magazine,* 2007.

Groom, Winston. "Saving New Orleans." *Smithsonian,* August 2006.

Hillig, Terry. "Researcher Says Jean Lafitte Is Buried in Alton Cemetery." *St. Louis Post-Dispatch,* February 10, 2000.

Hunter, Sue-Ann. "Famed Pirate Isn't Buried Here." *Alton (IL) Telegraph,* May 11, 1972.

Lafitte, Jean. *The Journal of Jean Lafitte: The Privateer-Patriot's Own Story.* New York: Vantage Press, 1958.

Laffite Society. "Biographical Notes from the Lafitte Society of Galveston, Texas." http://thelaffitesociety.com/index.html.

Leavell, Alfred, Jr. "An Early History of Alton, Illinois: 1817–1865." Master's thesis, Southern Illinois University at Edwardsville, 1966.

Maddox, Teri. "Searching for Jean Lafitte." *Belleville (IL) News-Democrat,* April 20, 2000.

Reeves, Sally. "Searching for Lafitte the Pirate." https://www.frenchquarter.com/jeanlaffitte.

Waley, Dave. "Research Finds Famed Pirate May Be Buried in Alton." *Alton (IL) Telegraph,* February 1, 2000.

An Abused Slave and the Woman Who Saved Him

Bauser, Beverly. "The Story of Jarret and the Woman Who Saved Him." Madison County ILGenWeb, www.facebook.com/madison.ilgenweb/posts/2108692505836084.

Klickna, Cinda. "Slavery in Illinois." Illinois Periodicals Online, https://www.lib.niu.edu/2003/ih090315.html.

New-York Historical Society and Museum. "When Did Slavery End in New York State?" https://www.nyhistory.org/community/slavery-end-new-york-state.

St. Louis History Blog. "Marine Villa's Lost Marine Hospital." https://stlouishistoryblog.com.

The First Duel in Illinois

Afflect, James. "The Stuart Bennett Duel." In *Transactions of the Illinois State Historical Society for the Year 1901*. Springfield, IL: Phillips Brothers, State Printers, 1901.

History of St. Clair County, Illinois. Philadelphia: Brink, McDonough and Company, 1881.

Missouri State Archives. "Crack of the Pistol: Dueling in 19th Century Missouri." https://www.sos.mo.gov/archives/education/dueling.

Moore, A.W. "Illinois Town—Early History." Illinois State Museum, http://www.museum.state.il.us/RiverWeb/landings/Ambot/Archives/fwp/Bloody_20Island.html.

Wilderman, A.A., and A.S. Wilderman. *Encyclopedia of Illinois and History of St. Clair County*. Vol. 2. Chicago: Munsell Publishing Company, 1907.

Tickets to a Black Abolitionist's Hanging

Buchanan, Thomas C. "Rascals on the Antebellum Mississippi: African American Steamboat Workers and the St. Louis Hanging of 1831." *Journal of Social History* 34, no. 4 (Summer 2001).

Chambers, A.B. *Trials and Confessions of Madison Henderson, alias Blanchard, Alfred Amos Warrick, James W. Seward, and Charles Brown, Murderers of Jesse Baker and Jacob Weaver, as Given by Themselves; and a Likeness of Each, Taken in Jail Shortly after Their Arrest*. St. Louis: Chambers and Knapp–Republican Office, 1841. E-edition published on the website Documenting the American South, https://docsouth.unc.edu.

Dunphy, John J. "Tickets to a Black Abolitionist's Hanging on a Mississippi River Island." St. Louis Post-Dispatch Book Blog, https://www.stltoday.com/entertainment/books-and-literature/book-blog, June 17, 2014.

Schneider, Paul. *Old Man River: The Mississippi River in North American History*. New York: Henry Holt and Company, 2013.

The Lincoln-Shields Duel

Angle, Paul M., and Earl Schenck Miers, eds. *The Living Lincoln*. New Brunswick, NJ: Rutgers University Press, 1955.

Dunphy, John J. "A Tale of Two Islands." *Illinois Magazine*, May–June 1983.

Lamon, Ward H. *The Life of Abraham Lincoln*. Lincoln: University of Nebraska Press, 1999.

Myers, James. *The Astonishing Saber Duel of Abraham Lincoln*. Springfield, IL: Lincoln-Herdon Building Press, 1968.

The Lynching of a Schoolteacher

Alton (IL) Evening Telegraph. "Race War Imminent." June 9, 1903.

Belleville New-Democrat. "County Superintendent of Schools Hertel Shot." June 6, 1903.

———. "Was Out Thursday." July 2, 1903.

Cha-Jua, Sundiata. *America's First Black Town: Brooklyn, Illinois, 1830–1915*. Urbana: University of Illinois Press, 2000.

Downey, Dennis B. "A 'Many Headed Monster': The 1903 Lynching of David Wyatt." *Journal of Illinois* 2, no. 1 (Spring 1999): 2–16.

Ingram, James. "Belleville aka Lynchville 200th Anniversary Not All Festive." *St. Louis American*, March 13, 2004.

Miller, Randall M. "Lynching in America: Some Context and a Few Comments." *Pennsylvania History: A Journal of Mid-Atlantic Studies* 72, no. 3 (2005): 275–91.

New York Times. "Illinois Lynching Horror." June 8, 1903.

St. Louis Post-Dispatch. "Action Urged by Belleville Citizens." June 23, 1903.

———. "Officers Fear No Inquiry Iito Lynching of Negro," June 12, 1903.

Strange Fruit and Spanish Moss. "June 6, 1903, David Wyatt." http://strangefruitandspanishmoss.blogspot.com/2014/06/june-6-1903-david-wyatt.html.

Wilderman, A.A., and A.S. Wilderman. *Encyclopedia of Illinois and History of St. Clair County*. Vol. 2. Chicago: Munsell Publishing Company, 1907.

The Brief but Wild History of Benbow City

Alton (IL) Evening Telegraph. "Amos E. Benbow Dies Following an Illness Lasting Three Years." November 15, 1922.
———. "Bad Fight at Benbow City and Wood River." November 7, 1908.
———. "Benbow Case Under Advisement." June 2, 1909.
———. "Benbow City Begins Licensing Saloons." May 4, 1908.
———. "How Wood River Got Its Start." September 27, 2008.
———. "Move for Annexation of Benbow to Wood River." July 9, 1909.
———. "New Post Office for Benbow City." October 3, 1908.
———. "Two More Saloons for Benbow City." September 14, 1908.
Dunphy, John J. "The Wide-Open Town of Benbow City." *Springhouse Magazine*, 2008.
Ford, Jesse W. "The Rise and Fall of Benbow City." *Wood River (IL) Journal*, November 7, 1974.
Hull, Herbert A. "Messenger and Allied Families." *Americana Illustrated* 20, no. 4 (1926).
Morwood, Burton Westlake. "A Modern Saga of an Old-Time Upper Alton Home." Unpublished paper about the Hurlbut-Messenger House, dated April 9, 1971, and in the possession of the author.
New York Times. "Saloon for Each Thirteen." May 5, 1908.
———. "Steal Marshal's Clothes: Benbow City Official in Doubt If Thieves Robbed Him in His Sleep." September 15, 1912.
Read, Roxann. *Wood River Along the River Bend*. Charleston, SC: Arcadia Publishing, 2003.

Curtis Reese: Minister, Humanist, Crimefighter

Alton (IL) Evening Telegraph. "Demands Protection from City of Alton." March 28, 1914.
———. "Installation of Dr. Reese a Big Success." November 14, 1913.
———. "Rev. C.W. Reese Beset by Gang of Gamblers at Mitchell." December 17, 1914.
———. "Unitarian Pastor Was Former Baptist." July 5, 1913.
———. "Will Hear New Preacher." April 11, 1913.
Dunphy, John J. "Famous Humanist Fought Crime in Alton." *Alton (IL) Telegraph*, October 5, 2008.

Forcade, Lottie. "A History of First Unitarian Church of Alton, 1836–1986." Unpublished paper housed in the library of First Unitarian Church of Alton.

Harvard Square Library. "Reese, Curtis W. (1887–1961)." https://www.harvardsquarelibrary.org/biographies/curtis-w-reese.

"Letters from the Family of a Man Who Had Changed." Manuscript housed in the Archives and Manuscript Library of Andover–Harvard Theological Library.

Olds, Mason. "Curtis Reese: Statesman of Religious Humanism, 1887–1961." Notable American Unitarians, https://web.archive.org/web/20051014014712/http://www.harvardsquarelibrary.org/unitarians/reese.html.

Reese, Curtis. *Humanism*. Chicago: Open Court Publishing Company, 1926.

———. *Humanist Religion*. New York: Macmillan, 1931.

Schulz, William F. *Making the Manifesto: The Birth of Religious Humanism*. Boston: Skinner House Books, 2002.

The East St. Louis Race Riot

Barnes, Harper. *Never Been a Time: The 1917 Race Riot That Sparked the Civil Rights Movement*. New York: Walker and Company, 2008.

———. "Racial Memory: Clear as Black and White." *Saint Louis Beacon*, June 28, 2008.

Dunphy, John J. "The East St. Louis Race Riot of 1917." *Springhouse Magazine*, 1992.

———. "New Light on the 1917 East St. Louis Race Riot." *Springhouse Magazine*, 2009.

———. "The Reasons for the Riot." *Alton (IL) Telegraph*, July 19, 2017.

Henderson, Jane. "From Riots to Civil Rights." *St. Louis Post-Dispatch*, June 29, 2008.

Lumpkins, Charles L. *American Pogrom: The East St. Louis Race Riot and Black Politics*. Athens: Ohio University Press, 2008.

Pollack, Joe. "East St. Louis Race Riot Remembered." *Belle Lettres* 9, no. 1 (September/December 2008).

Rudwick, Elliot M. *Race Riot at East St. Louis, July 2, 1917*. Carbondale: Southern Illinois University Press, 1964.

Theising, Andrew J. "Lessons of Race Riot Are Reassessed." *St. Louis Post-Dispatch*, November 2, 2008.

The Lynching of Robert Prager: A World War I Hate Crime

Dillard, Irving. Interview with the author, 1983.

Dunphy, John J. "Hate Crime during World War I Shows Government-Induced Hysteria." *Alton (IL) Telegraph*, October 5, 2005.

———. "The Lynching of Robert Prager." *Illinois Magazine*, May–June 1984.

———. "Murder at Midnight." *Springhouse Magazine*, April 1995.

———. "When Paranoia Turns Deadly." *St. Louis Post-Dispatch*, April 5, 1993.

Hickey, Donald. "The Prager Affair: A Study in Wartime Hysteria." *Journal of the Illinois State Historical Society* (Summer 1969).

Luebke, Frederick C. *Bonds of Disloyalty: German Americans and World War I.* DeKalb: Northern Illinois University Press, 1974.

Schwartz, E.A. "The Lynching of Robert Prager, the United Mine Workers, and the Problem of Patriotism in 1918." *Journal of the Illinois State Historical Society* (Winter 2003).

St. Louis Globe Democrat. "The Robert Prager Lynching: Media Reaction." April 5, 1918.

The Ku Klux Klan in Southwestern Illinois

Alton (IL) Evening Telegraph. "H.H. Lessner, Former Police Justice, Dead." July 13, 1925.

———. "K.K.K. Buys Wesley Church As Klan Home." January 16, 1924.

———. "Klan Funeral at Klavern For H.H. Lessner." July 17, 1925.

———. "Klan Unmasked at Funeral on Mayor's Order." July 20, 1925.

———. "Ku Klux Klan Holds Spectacular Meeting." June 7, 1924.

———. "Ku Klux Klan Was Active Briefly." July 2, 1976.

———. "On Ku Klux Klan By Rev. Townsend." February 25, 1924.

Bosworth, Charles, Jr., and Pat Gauen. "Klan Rally Draws Taunts, Jeers—Police, Barricade Contain Klansmen." *St. Louis Post-Dispatch*, May 7, 1994.

Boyd, Eldon. "Mayor: Diversity Is a Blessing." *Edwardsville (IL) Intelligencer*, May 7, 1994.

Candela, Shawn. "Onlookers Still See Bigotry, Reject New Klan Image." *Edwardsville (IL) Intelligencer*, May 7, 1994.

Carroll, Joe. "KKK Granted Permit for Rally." *Alton (IL) Telegraph*, March 29, 1994.

Chalmers, David M. *Hooded Americanism: The History of the Ku Klux Klan.* New York: New Viewpoints, 1981.

Dragich, Susan. "Hundred Expected at Unity Rally." *Alton (IL) Telegraph*, September 12, 1992.

———. "Klan Unlikely to Take Root Here, Writer Says." *Alton (IL) Telegraph*, September 15, 1992.

———. "Residents Are Urged to Ignore Klan Rally." *Alton (IL) Telegraph*, August 27, 1992.

———. "SIUE Groups Protests at Klan Gathering." *Alton (IL) Telegraph*, September 13, 1992.

Dunphy, John J. "Don't Give the Klan a Free Ride." *St. Louis Post-Dispatch*, February 21, 1994.

———. "KO the KKK." Letter to the editor, *St. Louis Post-Dispatch*, January 19, 1992.

———. "The Ku Klux Klan in Alton." *Springhouse Magazine*, 2008.

———. "Unity Rally Lives On in Minds of Participants." Letter to the editor, *Alton (IL) Telegraph*, September 25, 1992.

Gutowski, Christy. "Klan Rally Sparks Anti-Hate Drive." *Alton (IL) Telegraph*, February 20, 1994.

Hillery, Jason. "Unity Rally in Alton Outdraws Klan." *Alton (IL) Telegraph*, September 13, 1992.

Hillig, Terry. "Marchers Will Ignore Klan Rally." *Alton (IL) Telegraph*, March 31, 1994.

Jackson, Kenneth. *The Ku Klux Klan in the City, 1915–1930*. New York: Oxford University Press, 1967.

Jacobs, Dennis. "Opponent Sees Klan Rally as Being Counterproductive." *Alton (IL) Telegraph*, April 19, 1994.

Kulier, Jennifer. "OPIN Letter Offers View of Tolerance." *Edwardsville (IL) Intelligencer*, May 7, 1994.

Lichtman, Allan J. *White Protestant Nation: The Rise of the American Conservative Movement*. New York: Atlantic Monthly Press, 2008.

Lumpkins, Charles L. *American Pogrom: The East St. Louis Race Riot and Black Politics*. Athens: Ohio University Press, 2008.

Lutholtz, M. William. *Grand Dragon: D.C. Stephenson and the Ku Klux Klan in Indiana*. West Lafayette, IN: Purdue University Press, 1991.

Weller, Linda. "Edwardsville Is Ready for Klan, Walk of Commitment Friday." *Alton (IL) Telegraph*, May 5, 1994.

Wessol, Shay. "Klan Angers Crowd, Stirs Little Trouble." *Edwardsville (IL) Intelligencer*, May 7, 1994.

Western Catholic (Quincy, IL). "Right Rev. J.A. Griffin, D.D., Receives Great Ovation in Alton." June 13, 1924.

James Earl Ray and the Murder of Dr. Martin Luther King Jr.

Alton (IL) Evening Telegraph. "King Murder Revisited." June 19, 2000.

———. "'Ray Pulled Trigger.'" April 4, 1998.

———. "Ray's Dying Wish: Prove Innocence." April 24, 1998.

———. "Ray's Life of Crime Began in Alton." April 24, 1998.

———. "Service Held for Ray." May 29, 1998.

Dunphy, John J. "James Earl Ray." *Springhouse Magazine,* 2009.

———. "The Secret Revealed: How James Earl Ray Got His Money." *New Letters* 77, no. 2 (Winter 2011): 105–8.

Emery, Tom. "50 Years Later, Questions Remain about Alton Native Ray's Role in MLK Assassination." *Alton (IL) Telegraph,* April 4, 2018.

Huie, William Bradford. "The Story of James Earl Ray and the Plot to Assassinate Martin Luther King." *Look,* November 12, 1968.

Kramer, Roger. "Ray's Biography Declares 'Conspiracy.'" *Alton (IL) Telegraph,* March 31, 1988.

Levins, Harry. "Ray Spent Much of His Life in St. Louis Area, Getting into Trouble." *St. Louis Post-Dispatch,* April 24, 1998.

McWhirter, William A. "The Story of the Accused Killer of Dr. King." *Life,* May 3, 1968.

Yakstis, Ande. "Alton Bank Robbery Financed Ray's Escape." *Alton (IL) Telegraph,* April 4, 1998.

The Nike Missile Base at Pere Marquette State Park

Alton (IL) Evening Telegraph. "Denies Nike Base Ruins State Park." March 20, 1959.

———. "First Troops Due at Grafton Monday." July 17, 1959.

———. "He Sits Alone at Silent Nike." December 22, 1965.

———. "Open House Set Saturday at Missile Base." May 17, 1967.

———. "Road to Nike Base Widened." January 3, 1961.

———. "Sees Long Life for Nike Base." September 25, 1963.

Binder, Donald E. "The Nike Missile System: A Concise Historical Overview." National Investigations Committee on Aerial Phenomena, http://www.nicap.org/reports/nike4.htm.

Dunphy, John J. "The Nike Missile Base at Marquette Park." *Springhouse Magazine,* 2008.

Ed Thelen's Nike Missile Web Site, ed-thelen.org.

Hurly, Sue. "Then and Now, Work on Nike Missile Base Was a Family Affair." *Telegraph* (Alton, IL), June 16, 1993.

Niemeyer, Richard. E-mail to the author, May 9, 2008.

———. E-mail to the author, May 12, 2008.

Nike Historical Society, nikemissile.org.

ABOUT THE AUTHOR

B orn in Alton, Illinois, and now residing in the village of Godfrey, John J. Dunphy is a summa cum laude graduate of Southern Illinois University at Edwardsville and attended that university's graduate school on an academic fellowship. He taught writing at Lewis and Clark Community College for almost a decade and conducts numerous writers' workshops.

Dunphy's books include *Lewis and Clark's Illinois Volunteers*, *Unsung Heroes of the Dachau Trials: The Investigative Work of the U.S. Army 7708 War Crimes Group, 1945–1947* as well as two books for Arcadia/The History Press: *From Christmas to Twelfth Night in Southern Illinois* and *Abolitionism and the Civil War in Southwestern Illinois*. His poetry collections include *Touching Each Tree*, *Stellar Possibilities* and *Dark Nebulae*. He writes a weekly column for the *Telegraph* (Alton, IL). He has owned the Second Reading Book Shop in Alton since 1987. The bookstore's location served as an Underground Railroad station. Visit John J. Dunphy on Facebook.

Visit us at
www.historypress.com